*"The Torah is a commentary on the world,
and the world is a commentary on the Torah."*

Rabbi Shlomo Carlebach

Rav Kook's Introduction to
Shabbat Ha'aretz

Rav Kook's Introduction
to *Shabbat Ha'aretz*

Rabbi Abraham Isaac Kook

Translated and with an introduction
by Julian Sinclair

JEWISH INSPIRATION. SUSTAINABLE COMMUNITIES.

Hazon • New York
Copyright © 2014 by Hazon, Inc.

Published in the United States by Hazon, Inc.
This work is made available under the terms of the Creative Commons
Attribution-NonCommercial-ShareAlike License.
http://creativecommons.org/licenses/by-nc-sa/3.0/us/deed.en_US

Library of Congress Control Number: 2014937180

ISBN: 978-0-9912708-0-4

TABLE OF CONTENTS

FOREWORD:
WHY THIS BOOK, WHY NOW, AND FOR WHOM IS IT INTENDED?

Why now is the easiest of these questions. For too long, the shmita—sabbatical—year in Jewish life has been considered within too narrow a frame. Every seven years, there is an argument in Israel about the *heter mekhira* (the provision that was itself partly the trigger for *Shabbat Ha'aretz*), which enables a circumvention of the shmita rules in relation to growing food in the land of Israel. The modern orthodox, by and large, support it; the ultraorthodox, increasingly, oppose it; and those who are not orthodox observe this without much interest in, or respect for, the combatants or their arguments on either side.

This state of affairs is sad in and of itself. But the shame of it is made far worse when one starts to think about shmita in a wider contemporary frame. Shmita is a part of Jewish tradition that is remarkable in its breadth and salience. The provisions of shmita offer wisdom in relation to a considerable number of the most critical issues of our time: not just our relationship to land but also where our food comes from and to whom it goes, the nature of community, our understanding of the role of debt within a healthy society, the relationship between those who own land and those who do not, and the question of how we relate to time itself.

Shmita challenges us to think through a wide range of presumptions we hold in contemporary life. In the long-running argument between capitalism and socialism, for instance, the provisions and commentary of shmita are a challenge to both sides. To those who would be socialist or confiscatory, shmita comes to say: private ownership is a good and necessary thing; so, too, is the ability to lend or borrow money. To those who espouse a more unfettered capitalism, shmita comes with this critique: land ownership is relative, not absolute; and your entitlement to own land must be balanced, on a regular and periodic basis, with your responsibility to those in your community who are in need. The contemporary barbed-wire fence and its KEEP OUT signs have no place in the world imagined by shmita.

I make these observations to start to give a sense of the people for whom this book is intended.

It is certainly intended for you if you are Jewish and observant or learned. We hope that you will find it fascinating and that it will deepen your reverence for shmita as a concept in general and for the remarkable vision of Rav Kook in particular.

It is intended for you if you are Jewish but less observant or less knowledgeable. We hope that this book will give you a sense of how extraordinary shmita is and that it will lead you to further learning, reflection, and action.

It is a particularly fascinating text for those who are most universalistic within Jewish communities, including many who are idealistic in relation to the world and who chafe at a certain kind of particularism in Jewish life. Rav Kook in his life and in his writings saw a mystical significance in the Jewish connection to the land of Israel, and at least one group of his followers have extended that aspect of his thinking into the political realm to this day. They do not falsely imagine such an intense attachment to the land, the people, and the relationship between the two in the teachings of Rav Kook. The introduction to *Shabbat Ha'aretz* is suffused with a passionate sense of the spiritual possibilities opened up by the Jewish people's modern-day return to the land of Israel. But this—for me personally—makes Rav Kook's writings more, not less, salient. His writings challenge the Jewish community simultaneously in two opposing directions. Those who claim the most particularistic aspects of Rav Kook need to reckon with his intense sense of spirituality, his humility, and his deep reverence for all life. Those who are most universalistic should take a moment to think about the value of localism in the world today, the extent to which attachment to the world in general must be rooted in love for some particular corner of the planet, and the way that this love for the land of Israel has anchored the Jewish people through centuries of dispersion and inspires idealistic innovation to this day.

And that is why this book is intended for you also if you are a thoughtful Christian, or Muslim, or Hindu, or Buddhist—or of any other faith tradition. It may require of you a little Googling or a visit to Wikipedia or elsewhere, to look up some further contextual references. But we hope that you will find this book interesting and challenging. The role of religion is up for grabs on this planet right now. People have begun this century by murdering in the name of religion, just as in centuries gone by; yet those who do so are in a tiny minority of people of faith. The overwhelming majority of those who seek to engage their religious tradition do so with the belief that ancient wisdom is humane and that it speaks to us—it can and should speak to us—still to this day. I hope that as this century unfolds, the Jewish tradition of shmita may become an opportunity to learn and share among religious traditions of all sorts. What would a Tibetan Buddhist make of shmita? How does a Native American read Rav Kook? What would be a Sufi commentary on Rabbi Julian Sinclair's introduction? We hope that, in due course, some of these conversations will unfold. Their focus is not shmita itself but rather the world imagined by shmita, a world we have yet to bring to fruition—one that balances between land and people, between economic growth and the disequilibrium of inequality, and between the different interests of neighbors of all sorts.

Finally, this book is intended for you if you are of no religious tradition at all or have no interest in religion per se. Jewish tradition is too rich and interesting to be the sole province of Jews, and religious traditions are too vital but sometimes also too problematical to leave them only in the hands of believers. Those of you whose focus is not religion but, for instance, permaculture; land use; crop rotation; cohousing and intentional community; ecological restoration; transition towns; micro-finance; debt relief; social innovation; the renewal of cities; the nourishment of soil; the need to compost; transportation alternatives—if you are involved in any or all of these topics, or a hundred others, we hope that you will read this book, discuss it with your friends, teach it, critique it, and, most of all, engage deeply with it. Rav Kook was a mystic, but he was a remarkably practical mystic in some ways. The ancient wisdom of shmita, honored by Rav Kook, renewed by Julian and others, bears fruitful thought and action today and tomorrow.

At Hazon, we have been working on shmita fairly steadily since 2008. Our mission is to create a healthier and more sustainable Jewish community and a healthier and more sustainable world for all. At our website—hazon.org—you can see the range of our programs, which are now substantial. But our specific programs are only a part of our work. Above and beyond the specific things we do, there is a genuine belief that—in a phrase that I heard from Reb Shlomo Carlebach, z"l, in 1994—"*the Torah is a commentary on the world, and the world is a commentary on the Torah.*" These words are not self-evident, nor are they trite.

Our organizational mission can be accomplished in tangible ways—by providing transformational experiences for people as individuals, by supporting local organic farms, by helping to renew Jewish institutions, by strengthening the Israeli environmental movement, by advocating today or tomorrow for protected bike lanes or a more equitable farm bill or for healthier food policies in Jewish institutions. But the real measure of our success will be measured decades hence, and perhaps not for a century or two. Real change will come if we can shift even slightly the axis of what it means to be Jewish, so that to be Jewish is both to deepen our commitment to Torah, widely construed, and to engage more profoundly with the wider world. Too frequently in Jewish life, one of these two things seems to happen at the expense of the other.

That is the wider context for our work on shmita and this book. Rav Kook in his life and in his writings strove to weave together seemingly disparate entities. He treasured the individual, the community, the nation, and the whole world. It will be a fitting tribute to his memory and to his teaching if we advance that mission in what we do and in how we seek to do it.

Finally, some words of personal gratitude.

I very gratefully acknowledge the Opaline Fund, which has underwritten the production of this book.

I am immensely grateful to Hazon's staff, who are incredibly hardworking and amazingly idealistic and do so much good in the world each day. I thank our board members and supporters, who enable us to do this work, and I especially thank UJA-Federation of New York and the Lisa and Douglas Goldman Fund, whose support underwrote earlier parts of Hazon's work on shmita.

Of intellectual colleagues and fellow travelers, I have learned especially from Dr. Mirele Goldsmith, Rabbi David Ingber, Einat Kramer, Aharon Ariel Lavi, Amichai Lau-Lavie, Rav Michael Melchior, Deborah Newbrun, Orly Dabush Nitzan, Ran Raviv, Eran Shafir, and Yossi Tsuria. Very special thanks go to the remarkable Judith Belasco, who leads all of Hazon's thought-leadership work, this book included. Dr. Bonna Haberman, Rabbi

Micha Odenheimer, and Rabbi Ethan Tucker gave a remarkable session on shmita at Hazon's Food Conference, which I will not soon forget. Limor Friedman and Claire Nacamuli shepherded our Shmita Summit in London, where Julian first shared his work-in-progress on this book. I'm grateful to Canon Giles Fraser and Daniel Taub, whose participation in a panel at that Summit enlarged my own understanding of Shmita through an interfaith lens. Dr. Jeremy Benstein and Dyonna Ginsburg have become my beloved partners in Siach, a conversation that enriches its participants and that has nurtured much of this work on shmita. Yigal Deutscher, Anna Hanau, and Nati Passow helped bring *The Hazon Shmita Sourcebook* to fruition, which, in turn, made this book possible. Lauren Greenberg put in many hours to help make this book, in particular, a reality. To each and all of you: great thanks.

I want to thank especially three people without whom you would not be reading this work: Jorian Polis Schutz, Rabbi Julian Sinclair, and Elisheva Urbas. One of the central ideas of shmita is that much of what we own should really be shared—in its production and in its harvesting. That has been true in this process. Jorian is the person whose brilliant idea this originally was and who enabled this project to come to fruition. My confidence in proceeding with the project was grounded in knowing that, to a quite astonishing extent, Julian was uniquely placed to translate and explicate Rav Kook. Elisheva has shepherded the ideas and words of Jorian, Julian, and me to practical fruition with graciousness, start to finish. Elisheva, Julian, and Jorian are good friends of mine, and I am immensely lucky to know each of them and to have the excuse to work with them. To each and all of you: *rav todot*.

I'm writing this foreword during *sefirat ha'omer*, the counting of the omer. Its cycle of seven weeks of seven days is capped by the fiftieth, which is Shavuot, the festival of the giving of the Torah. This maps to the seven shmita cycles of seven years, capped by the fiftieth, which is *yovel*, the Jubilee. I have slowly understood that Jewish tradition is a fractal tradition: its elements apply at different levels of scale.

There is a beautiful instance of this in the Torah, both in what it says and in how we might read it. In enjoining shmita, the Torah also acknowledges how daunting its observance might seem: "*If you will say, what will we eat in the seventh year, for we have not planted or gathered our produce?*" (Vayikra/Leviticus 25:20). Jorian pointed out to me that in addition to being a literal question, this verse is also, in a sense, asking more broadly, *How can such a huge idea ever actually work?* It is the wisdom of the Torah and of Rav Kook—and, I think, the intuition of Jorian and of many of us who are working on shmita—that it is precisely by asking these questions that we reveal the blessings inherent in shmita and in the world.

Each moment and each unit of time are opportunities for what the tradition calls *k'fiyat yetzer*, the focusing of the will. As we publish this little book, and as you read it, I hope and pray that together we will learn from Rav Kook, from the tradition, and from one another, and that by doing so, we may create a healthier and more sustainable Jewish community and a healthier and more sustainable world for all.

Nigel Savage
New York, Lag b'Omer 5774

RAV KOOK AND THE MEANING OF SHMITA

Shabbat Ha'aretz, published by Rabbi Abraham Isaac Kook on the eve of the 1909–10 shmita year, is undoubtedly the most important and influential book on shmita to have appeared in the modern era. It is indispensable to understanding how shmita is currently observed and not observed. The context, arguments, and aftermath of *Shabbat Ha'aretz* remain formative forces upon the status of shmita in the State of Israel. There is probably no more important text for understanding why shmita is the way it is today.

But throughout *Shabbat Ha'aretz*, and particularly its introduction, shines a vision of how shmita could be much more than it is today. Rav Kook believed in the power of social and spiritual reawakening embodied in shmita. He hoped that the leniency that enabled the land to be sold and, effectively, shmita not to be observed was a step on the journey toward the renewal of shmita.

This introduction will outline some of the sources in Rav Kook's life and his work for his thinking on shmita, summarize the outlines of his halakhic argument in *Shabbat Ha'aretz*, and explore briefly the resources in Rav Kook's introduction to

Shabbat Ha'aretz that point beyond the *heter mekhira* compromise to a fuller and richer observance of shmita.

Shmita

Three passages in the Torah discuss shmita. Each passage reveals a different dimension of shmita's values and practices. Let us briefly examine each section in turn.

> *You shall not oppress a stranger, for you know the feelings of the stranger, having been yourselves strangers in the Land of Egypt. Six years shall you sow your land and gather in your yield; but in the seventh year, you shall let it rest and lie fallow. Let the needy among your people eat of it; and what they leave, let the wild beasts eat. You shall do the same with your vineyards and your olive groves. Six days you shall do your work; but on the seventh day, you shall cease from labor, in order that your ox and ass may rest and that your bondsman and stranger may be refreshed. (Exod. 23:10–12)*

The passage above focuses on the egalitarian aspect of shmita. In the seventh year, agricultural work ceases, and the produce of the land becomes ownerless. The poor and needy enter into previously private fields, vineyards, and olive groves and eat the crops. Animals may come and eat what is left. Property rights in the land and its produce are erased; rich and poor, humans and beasts all share what grows naturally in the shmita year. The verses about shmita are placed between the reminder not to oppress the stranger because we were once strangers in Egypt and a repetition of the command to keep Sabbath, which emphasizes the rights of your servants and animals to rest with you. This juxtaposition sites shmita in the context of the Torah's concern for the poor, the marginalized, and the oppressed.

> *When you enter into the land that I assign you, the land shall observe a Sabbath of the Lord. Six years you may sow your field, and six years you may prune your vineyard, and gather in the yield; but in the seventh year, the land shall have a Sabbath of complete rest, a Sabbath of the Lord: you shall not sow your field or prune your vineyard. You shall not reap the aftergrowth of your harvest or gather the grapes of your untrimmed vines. It shall be a year of complete rest for the land, but you may eat whatever the land will produce during its Sabbath—you, your male and female slaves, the hired and bound laborers who live with you, and your cattle and the beasts on your land may eat all its yield. (Lev. 25:2–7)*

The Torah repeats the command to cease agricultural work in the seventh year, but the focus in the passage above is not on the poor but on the land. Just as people enjoy Sabbath one day out of seven, so, too, should the land have its Sabbath, one year out of seven. This is our duty of stewardship to the earth. We should not treat it as merely a resource to be perpetually exploited for our benefit; the land must also rest. During the land's Sabbath, we do not plant or cultivate it, and we eat only what grows by itself. Thus we show that we are not the land's ultimate masters. In this year, land is a place where humans, animals, and the earth itself meet on equal terms; there are no owners or exploiters but only fellow creatures.

> *Every seventh year, you shall practice remission of debts. This shall be the nature of the remission: every creditor shall remit the due that he claims from his fellow; he shall not exact payment from his fellow or kinsman, for the remission proclaimed is of the Lord. You may exact payment from the foreigner, but you must remit whatever is due you from the kinsman.... If, however, there is a needy person among you, one of your kinsmen in any of your settlements in the land that the Lord your God is giving you, do not harden your heart or shut your hand against your needy kinsman. Rather, you must open your heart and lend him sufficient for whatever he needs. Beware, lest you harbor the base thought, the seventh year, the year of remission is approaching, so that you are mean to your needy kinsman and give him nothing. He will cry out to the Lord against you, and you will incur guilt. Give to him readily, and have no regrets when you do so, for in turn, the Lord your God will bless you in all your efforts and all your undertakings. (Deut. 15:1–3; 7–10)*

The passage above adds a further dimension of shmita: the remission of debts. Every seven years, debts are canceled. The crushing obligations of debtors that weigh them down and can permanently cripple their flourishing are lifted. (It may be meritorious for the debtor to repay the loan after the shmita year, if he can, but he does not have to do so.) The Torah warns potential lenders against the suspicions that they may harbor of moral hazard in this situation. As the seventh year approaches, they should not withhold loans out of fear that the shmita will wipe out the debt. Rather, they must know that lending to the needy is among the responsibilities of the propertied, in full knowledge that the sabbatical debt remission may intervene to cancel the loan.

Jubilee

The Torah describes the Jubilee as the culmination of seven cycles of shmita observance:

> You shall count off seven weeks of years—seven times seven years—so that the period of seven weeks of years gives you a period of forty-nine years. Then you shall sound the horn loud; in the seventh month, on the tenth day of the month—the Day of Atonement—you shall have the horn sounded throughout your land, and you shall hallow the fiftieth year. You shall proclaim release throughout the

> *land for all its inhabitants. It shall be a Jubilee for you:*
> *each of you shall return to his holding, and each of you shall*
> *return to his family. That fiftieth year shall be a Jubilee*
> *for you: you shall not sow, and neither shall you reap the*
> *aftergrowth nor harvest the untrimmed vines, for it is a*
> *Jubilee. It shall be holy to you: you may eat only the growth*
> *direct from the field. In this year of Jubilee, each of you shall*
> *return to his holding. (Lev. 25:8–13)*

The Jubilee, which crowns seven seven-year shmita cycles, is a kind of super-sabbatical year. In addition to ceasing agricultural work, Hebrew slaves go free and every person returns to his ancestral holdings—meaning the piece of land that his family held when Joshua divided up the Land of Israel on entering the land 3,000 years ago. Whatever gains and losses in land holdings may have occurred over the previous fifty years, whether through good or bad luck, alacrity or laziness, talent or foolishness, were all erased. There was a society-wide reset as each family returned to its original patrimony. Accumulated socioeconomic advantages could not be passed down indefinitely to one's descendants; with the restoration of land, each family was returned to an original position of dignity and opportunity.

The shmita and Jubilee commandments are immensely radical. They legislate a septennial time-out in Jewish economic life, a year of spiritual renewal, a holiday for the land, a yearlong cease-fire in the economic struggle of all against all, an abolition of many of the rights of private property, a leveling of rich and poor, man and beast, earth and earth-dwellers, an amnesty on debt and, every half-century, a reset on the vicissitudes of the free market. These mitzvot represent a periodic challenge to the whole socioeconomic order. As Gerald Blidstein put it in an important article: "We have here more than the commonplace struggle between a radical religious demand and an unconsenting world. Rather, we have here an institution that contests the legitimacy of that world."[1]

So it is not surprising that the history of these commandments has been marked by conflict between their exacting requirements and the demands of economic reality. Indeed, it is remarkable that shmita was observed as diligently and for as long as it was. There is strong evidence that the sabbatical for the land was observed throughout the Second Temple period. At the famous assembly described by Nehemiah on their return to Israel in 516 BCE, the Jews took upon themselves the observance of shmita (Neh. 10:32). Among the many sources testifying that they generally did so is an account in Josephus's *Antiquities* of Alexander the Great reaching Jerusalem and acceding to the high priest's request that the Jews be exempt from paying tribute during the sabbatical year, when they did not work the land.[2] Numerous tannaitic sources attest that Jews in Israel continued to observe shmita for centuries after the destruction of Jerusalem

---

1 Gerald Jacob Blidstein, "Man and Nature in the *Sabbatical* Year," Tradition 9, no. 4 (1966): 50.

2 Josephus, *Antiquities* 11:338, quoted in *Encyclopaedia Judaica* 14:583.

by the Romans. After most Jews were exiled, shmita for the land (*shmitat karka'ot*) lapsed, as it is binding only on Jews living in the Land of Israel.

The remission of debts (*shmitat kesafim*), though technically binding inside and outside Israel, became largely moot from the first century BCE. Hillel the Elder saw that people were doing exactly what the Torah had warned them not to do: they were withholding loans in the run-up to the shmita year. The poor suffered most from people's reluctance to lend them money, an unintended consequence of a law that was meant to help them. So Hillel instituted the famous *prozbul* enactment, which handed over the responsibility for outstanding debts to the courts, which, as a public authority, were allowed to collect debts. Thus, observance of *shmitat kesafim* may be avoided. As for the Jubilee, according to most traditional sources, its practice ceased sometime during the First Temple period, when two and a half of the twelve tribes were exiled,[3] and there is some doubt as to whether the Jubilee was ever properly observed.

Maimonides writes, in his account of the messianic era at the end of the *Mishne Torah*, that among the many enactments to be expected of the Messiah, he will "cause the *shmitot* and the Jubilees to be observed as they are commanded in the Torah,"[4] clearly implying that they will not be fully observed until the Messiah comes. Rav Kook also implies this in *Shabbat Ha'aretz*.

---

3 Talmud Bavli, Arakhin 32b.

4 Maimonides, *Mishne Torah, Hilkhot Melakhim*, 11:1.

Only then will the socioeconomic order make space to fully honor these mitzvot, which radically question its legitimacy. The *heter mekhira* controversy has been the main modern arena for this clash between the demands of shmita and the exigencies of economic life and the principal modern test of the pre-messianic viability of shmita. The controversy was inextricably bound up with the life, times, and thought of Rabbi Abraham Isaac Kook.

Life of Rav Kook[5]

Rabbi Abraham Isaac Kook was born in Grieva, a small town in Lithuania, in 1865. His father, Shlomo Zalman ha-Cohen Kook, was descended from a distinguished rabbinical family and studied at the Volozhin yeshiva, the greatest academy of talmudic learning and piety in nineteenth-century Europe. His mother, Perel Zlota, came from a Chabad Hasidic family. She had imbibed the mystical passion of Hasidism and maintained her connection to Chabad after her marriage. When the third Lubavitcher rebbe, Menachem Mendel Schneerson, died in 1866, she received a button and some threads from his cloak, which she sewed into the skullcap of her eldest son, Abraham Isaac. Later in life, Rav Kook remarked to one of his students that

---

5 I was fortunate to benefit from prepublication access to Yehudah Mirsky's outstanding new biography of Rav Kook, which surpasses previous attempts to write about Rav Kook's life. See Mirsky, *Rav Kook: Mystic in a Time of Revolution* (New Haven, Conn.: Yale University Press, 2014). This biographical sketch is highly indebted to Mirsky's book, and statements in this section that are not otherwise attributed may be assumed to be from there.

his parents used to argue whether he would become an ascetic Mitnagdic rabbi in the Volozhin mold or a Hasidic master. In any event, he was able to integrate both models into his complex and multifaceted personality.

Abraham Isaac was recognized early on as a prodigy of rabbinic learning. From a young age, he studied alone or with private tutors, soon mastering the Talmud and Jewish law. At age fifteen, he left home to study in the *beit midrash* of Litsin, where he encountered maskilim (Jews who had absorbed the ideas of the European Enlightenment). He began to write verse and speak rich and precise grammatical Hebrew like a maskil. He then spent a year and a half studying in the Volozhin yeshiva, where he stood out for his learning and piety. Among Kook's fellow students at Volozhin were Micha Yosef Berdyczewski, who became a leading figure of Hebrew literature, and Chaim Nachman Bialik, later the national poet of Israel.

After Volozhin, Abraham Isaac married Batsheva Rabinowitz-Teomim. Compelled by poverty to seek a rabbinical position, he found employment as rabbi of Zoimel, a small town near the border with Latvia. In 1889, his wife died of pneumonia, leaving a baby daughter. Though devastated by grief, he quickly remarried his wife's cousin, with whom he had three more children. However, he continued to mourn his first wife for years afterward. During this period, he studied kabbalah intensively with the renowned scholar Rabbi Shlomo Elyashiv.

In 1896, Kook became rabbi of Boisk, a city of some 10,000 people. Boisk had a relatively well-off and educated Jewish community. During this period, Rav Kook expanded his studies of literature and philosophy. Though the sources of his secular education are unclear, we know that he was familiar with the main currents of modern European thought, citing Spinoza, Kant, Schopenhauer, and Nietzsche, among others, in his writings.

Throughout the 1890s, he sought a Jewish language in which to give expression to his rich inner world. He began a commentary on the *Ein Ya'akov*, a sixteenth-century compilation of the aggadic (nonlegal) parts of the Talmud. The aggadah, being less systematic and structured than the halakhic parts of the Talmud, allowed for a more expressive religious vocabulary. Rav Kook was also engaged with the Musar controversy, which was shaking the Eastern European yeshivot at that time. Musar was a movement of ethical revival, pioneered by Rabbi Israel Salanter, but it attracted criticism for the excesses of emotional exhortation and self-criticism of its followers. Rav Kook saw something valuable in the intense inwardness of Musar but believed that for it to be most effective, Musar needed to be studied from a text that one wrote oneself from the teachings nearest to one's soul.

After 1896, when Theodor Herzl convened the First Zionist Congress in Basel, the possibilities of a political return to Zion began to preoccupy Rav Kook. Between 1901 and 1904, he published a series of essays through which he emerged as a supporter of Jewish nationalism, albeit with some qualifications. Rav Kook was disturbed by the antireligious impulse that he saw in the nascent Zionist movement and argued that if Zionism remained divorced from religion, it would degenerate into mere nationalistic chauvinism.

In 1902, Yoel Moshe Salamon, a leading figure in the nascent Jewish settlements in Palestine, visited Boisk, seeking a new rabbi for Jaffa, an ancient town with a rapidly growing Jewish population that was becoming the urban hub of the new agricultural communities. Salamon was much taken with Rav Kook, and, shortly after his visit, the Jaffa search committee offered Rav Kook the post. Despite Kook's growing stature in the European rabbinate and Jaffa's reputation as "a place of desolate sin," he accepted the opportunity to play a formative role in the development of the Jewish community in Israel. He arrived in Jaffa on May 13, 1904.

The Jewish population in the Land of Israel at that time was divided into two opposing groups. One group was the Old Yishuv, comprising staunchly traditional Orthodox Jews who had emigrated during the nineteenth century for religious reasons—to study Torah and pray in the Holy Land. This community did not see itself as responsible for the economic and physical building of the land but subsisted almost entirely on a system of donations from Jews in the Diaspora, known as the *halukah*. The other group comprised Zionist pioneers of the New Yishuv. The wave of immigration beginning in 1882 known as the First Aliyah had been predominantly religious, but the Second Aliyah, beginning in 1904, was composed mainly of secular immigrants motivated by a mixture of Marxism, social democracy, Nietzschean notions of self-realization, and rebellion against Jewish tradition and the pioneers' bourgeois family backgrounds. Their goal was to create "normal" economic structures, thriving independently and supporting themselves by their own labor. The Old Yishuv regarded the pioneers of the New Yishuv as dangerous heretics dedicated to destroying traditional Jewish life. The New Yishuv, for its part, regarded the Old as primitive throwbacks to everything they hated about Diaspora Jewish life. David Ben-Gurion, who arrived with the Second Aliyah, charged that the leaders of the Old Yishuv "annihilate every free idea and crush every attempt for liberation…. This sector is dead and buried [and is] a population of obscurantists and schnorrers."[6] Spanning the chasm between these factions became a defining task of Rav Kook's life.

Rav Kook admired the pioneers' dedication and self-sacrifice in building the country and was excited by the redemptive possibilities of Jewish farmers planting the Land of Israel. Soon after his arrival, he toured the surrounding agricultural settlements, including Rishon l'Tzion, Nes Tziona, and Gedera, remarking to a friend: "I could kiss every stone of this holy land." He also shared much of the new immigrants' critique of the Old Yishuv, writing that "the vitality of the New Yishuv … cannot bear to see the hunched back, the drawn and melancholy face,

---

6 David Ben-Gurion, "On the Question of the Old Yishuv," *Ha'aḥdut* (1910): 2, quoted in Benjamin Ish-Shalom, *Rav Avraham Itzhak HaCohen Kook: Between Rationalism and Mysticism*, trans. Ora Wiskind-Elper (Albany: SUNY Press, 1993), 15.

that summons despair and faintness of heart, the vague eyes and the despair and hatred of life behind them."[7]

At the same time, Rav Kook was pained by the pioneers' rejection of Jewish tradition. He crystallized his ambivalence in a famous essay, "The Present Generation," in which he wrote: "Our generation is wondrous, a generation full of puzzlement. One is hard-pressed to find anything like it in all our history. It is composed of opposites, darkness and light groping about in confusion. It is low and degraded, and great and exalted; it is entirely guilty and entirely innocent."[8] He dreamed of a synthesis between the vitality of the New Yishuv and the commitment to tradition of the Old Yishuv. Rav Kook attempted to engage the secular writers and artists who were his neighbors in the Neve Tzedek area of Jaffa, with mixed success. Shai Agnon, who later won the Nobel Prize in Literature, had a regular *ḥavruta* with Rav Kook and became a lifelong admirer; Yosef Chaim Brenner, a mordant and saturnine observer of Diaspora Jewish life and regarded by many of his contemporaries as a sort of secular saint, was more guarded, praising Rav Kook as a "stormy and yearning soul" but scorning the "confused assumptions and untenable visions" of the latter's religious worldview.[9]

Shabbat Ha'aretz was written amid the controversy about

---

7 *Igerot hare'aya*, 1:185, quoted in Ish-Shalom, *Rav Avraham Itzhak HaCohen Kook*, 21.

8 "Hador," in *Eder hayakar* (Jerusalem: Mossad Harav Kook, 1967), 108.

9 Yosef Chaim Brenner, in *Hapo'el Hatza'ir* 40 (1910), quoted in Ish-Shalom, *Rav Avraham Itzhak HaCohen Kook*, 23.

shmita observance that shook the Yishuv in 1909. The roots of the dispute lay back in 1888, the first shmita year after the beginning of the First Aliyah. This wave of immigration, beginning in 1882, brought some 60,000 mostly religious Jews from Eastern Europe to live in the Yishuv. Unlike the traditionalists of the Old Yishuv, who subsisted on charitable donations from Europe, the newcomers worked the land. They endured poverty, starvation, malaria, and horrific rates of infant mortality as they struggled to eke out a living from agriculture.

With the advent of the shmita of 1888–89, it was clear to the pioneers that observing the sabbatical year as commanded in the Bible would be economically ruinous and would likely lead to the extinction of the nascent agricultural settlements. For a solution, they appealed to European rabbis, including Rabbi Shmuel Mohliver, who ruled that they might continue to work the land in the sabbatical year, provided that the land was sold to non-Jews for the duration of the shmita. This leniency was patterned after the permission to sell *ḥametz*, leavened food, to non-Jews during Passover in order to avoid serious financial loss. It was endorsed by Rabbi Yitzchak Elchanan Spektor of Kovno, the leading halakhic authority of the late nineteenth century.

The *heter mekhira*, as it became known, was seen as a temporary expedient. It was renewed for the shmita years of 1895–96 and 1902–3, each time amid bitter criticism from the Old Yishuv, which was not engaged in agriculture and saw the *heter* as a specious device for avoiding a biblical commandment.

By the shmita of 1909–10, the agrarian settlements had grown in scope and scale but still could not have survived the rigors of full shmita observance. Moreover, they had begun to export agricultural produce. They would lose these markets through ceasing work for a year and would probably be unable to recover them. A further difference this time around was that the religious farmers of the First Aliyah had now been augmented by the secularists of the Second Aliyah, who had no intention of taking a year off in the shmita.

Rav Kook's close identification with the pioneers led him to strongly endorse the *heter mekhira*. He argued in the face of opposition from rabbis in the Diaspora that only through direct knowledge of the suffering and self-sacrifice of the Zionist farmers could one truly understand what was at stake. Furthermore, the very viability of Judaism in the renewed Yishuv was on the line. If the halakhah could provide no solution to the most pressing existential needs of the farmers, they would turn their backs on Judaism in droves. He argued that if the rabbis showed themselves to be oblivious to the most basic needs of life the result would be the destruction of Torah and the abandonment of mitzvot.

In the summer of 1909, Rav Kook threw himself into educational activity around the issue of shmita in general and the *heter mekhira* in particular, culminating in the composition of *Shabbat Ha'aretz*, a densely argued 120-page work (written in just a week) that provided the most thorough, learned, and audacious justification for the *heter* that had ever been made.

The publication of *Shabbat Ha'aretz* ratcheted the controversy up to a new level. Rav Kook's most determined and prominent adversary was Rav Ya'akov David Willowsky (known as the "Ridbaz"), the rabbi of Tzfat, who had emigrated from Chicago in 1905. The Ridbaz opined that the sale of the *heter mekhira* was entirely fictional and made no difference to the status of the land. He purchased a small plot of land in the Galilee on the eve of the 1909–10 shmita just so that he could let it lie fallow. He accused Rav Kook of having been duped by his sympathy for the secular settlers into supporting the blatant transgression of one of the Torah's commandments. The two continued a polemical correspondence almost until the Ridbaz's death, in 1913. Rav Kook urged the Ridbaz to see that this was the generation that the Zohar called "good within but rotten without," which would build the material basis for redemption and required the support of rabbinic leaders to accomplish. The Ridbaz, a Lithuanian legal scholar to the core, saw only an egregious violation of the integrity of the Torah and was "unmoved by mystical attempts to find hidden light in everyone and everything."[10] Rav Kook refused to return in kind the often personal attacks of his detractors. He reaffirmed his belief that he and his critics were both arguing *l'shem shamayim*—for the sake of vital religious principles.

In November 1913, Rav Kook embarked on his most ambitious practical effort to build bridges to the New Yishuv. Together with a small group of rabbis, including Yosef Chaim

---

10 Mirsky, *Rav Kook*, 76.

Sonnenfeld, the leading authority of the Old Yishuv at the time, he set out on a monthlong trip to visit all the agricultural communities in the center and north of the country. The goals of the trip were to engage the pioneers in dialogue and strengthen Jewish education and the mitzvot connected to the land (tithes, first fruits, and so on). The rabbis met with enthusiastic responses in more traditional First Aliyah settlements such as Zikhron Ya'akov and Hadera but with more varied receptions in the strongholds of the Second Aliyah. In Merhavia, the workers virtually chased the rabbis out of the communal kitchen. Rav Kook calmly responded: "We have not come to influence you but rather to be influenced by your tremendous sacrifice on behalf of the Land of Israel."[11] At Poriya, overlooking the Sea of Galilee, Rav Kook took off his black coat and donned a watchman's cloak and head-scarf to dance with the pioneers, demonstrating his sense of kinship with them, beneath their very different garbs.[12]

In the summer of 1914, when Rav Kook and his wife were traveling to the Agudat Yisrael conference in Germany, the First

---

11 This is a well-known anecdote, quoted in a film about Rav Kook's life that is shown at Beit Harav, his house in Jerusalem. I have not been able to find a written source. The story of Rav Kook's 1913 journey is recounted in detail in Yonatan Binyamin Halevi Horowitz, *Eleh masei* (Jerusalem: Oraita, 2001). Horowitz accompanied Rav Kook on the trip and wrote his account in 1915.

12 This story is related in a letter dated September 1972, from Avraham Rosenblatt, a Tel Aviv accountant who had been present at Poriya during Rav Kook's 1913 visit, to Rabbi Yisrael Meir Lau, then chief rabbi of Tel Aviv. A facsimile of the letter is published in the sourcebook *L'an atah holeḥ* (Jerusalem: Beit Harav Kook, 2013).

World War broke out. The Kooks took refuge for a year and a half in Saint Gallen, Switzerland, where Rav Kook met David Cohen (known as "the Nazir" because he had sworn not to cut his hair or drink wine), a philosophy student who later became Kook's closest disciple. In search of a spiritual master, Cohen had traveled to meet Kook. After several hours of philosophical discussion, Cohen had been unconvinced as to whether this was indeed his rebbe, but the next morning, when he overheard Rav Kook praying, he knew that he had found what he had sought. "I listened," he later wrote, "and I was turned upside-down and became a different man."

In January 1916, Rav Kook moved to London to become rabbi of the Machzikei Hadath Orthodox synagogue on Brick Lane, in the East End. There, Rav Kook gathered an eclectic community of Hasidim, tailors, intellectuals, and East End radicals. He signed numerous rabbinic-ordination certificates to save young Jews from conscription (earning a stern warning from Scotland Yard). He also found time to frequent the National Gallery, becoming especially fond of Rembrandt. Rav Kook confided in an interview to the *Jewish Chronicle* that Rembrandt was one of the few tzaddikim who was privileged to see in this world the pure light that, according to a midrash, God stored up for the righteous in the world to come.[13]

While in London, Rav Kook became involved in public debates around the Balfour Declaration, championing the

---

13 Avram Melnikoff, "Rav Kook on Art," *Jewish Chronicle*, September 13, 1935.

centrality of the Land of Israel in Judaism against those assimilated British Jews who opined that the idea of Jewish nationhood was a biblical anachronism. The announcement of the declaration, in November 1917, electrified the religious Jewish world and roused Rav Kook to "old-new thoughts of spiritual and practical work" that he had dreamed of accomplishing in Israel. As the war drew to a close, he began to seek ways to return home. At the same time, the secular Zionists were looking for a reasonable rabbi to confer religious legitimacy on Zionism; and moderate rabbis in Jerusalem, led by Zvi Pesach Franck, were attempting to find a leader who would be a counterweight to the ultraorthodox. These different search paths converged on Rav Kook, who was offered the position of chief rabbi of Jerusalem in 1919. He returned to the holy city in late August of that year to assume the role.

In the postwar Yishuv, nation-building supplanted ideological discussion as the focus of the Jewish communities. As Yehudah Mirsky astutely points out, this shift left Rav Kook at a disadvantage. His unique ability to intellectually bridge and unite various Jewish groups far outstripped his skills in building or running organizations. He never developed a political or cultural base that could hold its own in the evolving ecosystem of Jewish institutions that became the nucleus of the future state. He envisioned the creation of a chief rabbinate that would lead the spiritual renaissance of the Jewish people in its land and take its place alongside the Hebrew University, the Zionist Executive, and other national institutions in waiting.

The secular Zionists supported an altogether more modest chief rabbinate that would deliver religious services and dampen intra-Jewish tensions while remaining firmly under the secular Zionists' control. The British—who were, by then, running the country—wanted a single Jewish address to turn to for religious matters (though they ended up with two—one Ashkenazi and one Sephardi); they convened an assembly that unanimously voted in Rav Kook as first chief rabbi of Palestine, in February 1921. The Old Yishuv, still deeply suspicious of Rav Kook's unconventional views and outreach to the secular, refused to recognize the chief rabbinate's authority. Mirsky summarizes the theory and practice of Rav Kook's chief rabbinate: "He sought to restore the great lawmaking bodies of classical Judaism and realize Maimonides' vision of halakhic constitutionalism, and what he got was a chronically underfunded, politically orphaned clerical bureaucracy."[14]

In his final years, Rav Kook was revered by the Yishuv (with the exception of some ultraorthodox zealots who continued to revile him until his death and, indeed, after it) as a spiritual giant. He was a courageous moral voice who spoke out against the British authority's supine inaction during the 1929 massacres of Jews by Arabs and against the British restrictions on Jews praying at the Western Wall. He championed the innocence of Abraham Stavsky and Abba Achimeir, Revisionist Zionists who were accused of murdering the Labor Zionist leader Chaim

14 Mirsky, *Rav Kook*, 235.

Arlosoroff in 1933, a cause célèbre that convulsed the whole Yishuv; Stavsky and Achimeir were subsequently acquitted.

Rav Kook died of cancer on September 1, 1935. Memorial services were held for him all over Palestine and in Jewish communities around the world. At one gathering, Bar-Ilan (a Religious Zionist leader and son of the Netziv, Rav Kook's *rosh yeshiva* in Volozhin) eulogized him: "Rav Kook loved the Jewish people, the way only a father can love his children. Nobody is left after him who will love the nation that fiercely.... He understood his people, the situation of the generation and its life conditions, and that is why he forgave them everything."

Thought

Rav Kook was one of the most important and influential Jewish thinkers of all time. His ideas are indispensable for understanding the state of Israeli politics and religion today. His immense body of writings includes profound and often startlingly original treatments of all the subjects that traditional Jewish thinkers concerned themselves with (as well as many that they did not), including God, revelation, Torah, commandments, halakhah, prayer, personal authenticity, art, science, evolution, socialism, nationalism, universalism, and messianism. In the face of this vast work, the following overview will merely summarize the areas of his thinking that are most relevant for understanding Rav Kook's thought about shmita.

Kabbalah

Scholars generally agree that kabbalistic mysticism was the backbone of Rav Kook's worldview (although they disagree over the extent to which his ideas were also influenced by the European thinking of his time). Rav Kook saw the universe as permeated with divine light. In the words of a classic passage from the Zohar, which he often quoted: "There is no place that is empty of Him, either above or below" (*Tikunei haZohar* 59). Godliness animates all ideas, people, and creatures. "There is a spark of divine light in all things."[15]

This vision was based on the teachings of Lurianic kabbalah, the masterly systematization of Jewish mysticism achieved by Rabbi Isaac Luria (1534–72) and his students. Lurianic kabbalah teaches that at the moment of Creation, infinite divine light was poured into "vessels," which, unable to withstand the intensity, shattered, scattering fragments of divine light everywhere. Much of the light became encased in *kelipot*—impure husks and shells that captured the sparks and prevented them from shining. This is the world we live in, full of trapped fragments of light. The goal of Jewish spiritual service—particularly the service of the tzaddikim, the truly righteous—is to identify, liberate, and raise up the hidden sparks.

For Rav Kook, the divine light of truth could be found almost anywhere: "This concept of tolerance is aware that there

---

15 "Concerning the Conflict of Beliefs and Opinions," in *Abraham Isaac Kook*, trans. Ben Zion Bokser (New York: Paulist Press, 1978), 273.

is a spark of divine light in all things, that the inner spark of divine light shines in all the different religions, as so many different pedagogics for the culture of humanity, to improve the spiritual and material existence, the present and future of the individual and of society."[16] To be sure, he was no relativist, and he emphatically declared that divine light was most fully present in the Torah, the revelation nurtured by the Jewish people. But he regarded the opinion that there is no truth outside Torah as "a frightful blindness" and taught that "the heart must be filled with love for all."[17]

Secularism

Rav Kook's embrace of the secular pioneers must be understood in light of this worldview. These pioneers were rebels against tradition and deniers of core Jewish beliefs; yet Rav Kook saw in their love and self-sacrifice on behalf of the Jewish people and the Land of Israel a blazing fire of divine light. He believed that Providence had chosen them to be the agents for the rebuilding and renaissance of Jewish life. The socialist and secular-nationalist ideologies in which they clothed their passion were, for Rav Kook, *kelipot* that would eventually fall away.

This attitude was radical enough to earn him the enmity of Orthodox factions, who could see nothing but heresy in secular Zionism. But Rav Kook went even further. In a seminal essay,

---

16 Ibid.

17 "The Moral Principles: Love," in Bokser, *Abraham Isaac Kook*, 135.

"The Souls of Chaos," Rav Kook implies that the idealistic rebels of the Second Aliyah were greater and closer to the divine light than many adherents of tradition: "The great idealists seek an order so firm and pure, beyond what may be found in the world of reality…. The souls inspired by the realm of chaos are greater than the souls whose affinity is with the established order. They are very great; they seek too much from existence, what is beyond their own faculties to assimilate. They seek a very great light."[18] The exalted stature and aspirations of such souls lead them into conflict with more prescribed and limited visions of goodness.

The pioneers' impatience with tradition manifested itself in chutzpah. In addition to being a Jewish folk characteristic, chutzpah is also a term of art with talmudic and kabbalistic antecedents. In "The Present Generation," Rav Kook wrote that the key to understanding the secularists was the strange talmudic statement from Mishnah Sotah 9:15, *b'ikveta demashiḥa ḥutzpa yasgei* ("In the time of the footsteps of the Messiah, chutzpah will grow").[19] Their rebellion against received ideas, norms, and behavior reflected a deeper attunement to the mighty messianic ideals that would be revealed in the imminent future.

For all the esteem in which he held the pioneers, Rav Kook was also grieved by their dismissal of tradition and believed that their idealism would fizzle and come to nothing if it remained divorced from the time-trodden paths to morality and holiness

---

18 "The Souls of Chaos," in Bokser, *Abraham Isaac Kook*, 256.

19 "Hador," 109.

represented by the life of Torah and mitzvot. He was impelled to engage with them even where other rabbinic leaders were repelled. Explaining his position, he wrote at the end of "The Souls of Chaos": "These passionate souls reveal their strength so that no fence can hold them back; and the weaklings of the established order, who are guided by balance and propriety, are too terrified to tolerate them.... But in truth, there is no need to be terrified.... Truly heroic spirits know that this force is one of the phenomena needed for the perfection of the world, for strengthening the power of the nation, of man, and of the world. Initially, this force represents the realm of the chaotic. But in the end, it will be taken from the wicked and turned over to the hands of the righteous."[20] As one of the "truly heroic spirits," Rav Kook felt driven to bridge the old and new, secular and traditional, pioneers and pietists, to demonstrate the beauty and relevance of Judaism to the secularists and the great-souled of the secularists to the religious.

Nationalism and Zionism

Rav Kook's relationship to Zionism was passionately supportive, yet conditional. He believed that the flowering of Jewish life in the Land of Israel that Zionism had inspired was nothing less than the beginning of the messianic redemption. "So shall it be in our days," he wrote in a letter, "as a result of our strengthening of the growing Yishuv ... the light of redemption and salvation

---

20 "The Souls of Chaos," 258.

will flourish."[21] He (unlike some of his followers) did not attempt to predict how long the "beginning" would last but was certain that the physical rebuilding and planting being done by the Zionist pioneers would eventually serve as a basis for the spiritual renaissance and transformation of the Jewish people and the universal redemption of all humankind.

This view was highly unconventional at the time and differed markedly from the stands of the traditionalists of the Old Yishuv and also the mainstream Religious Zionists of the Mizrachi movement. For the traditionalists, Zionism was a heresy that violated the implicit contract of the exile set out in the classic passage of the "Three Oaths" (Talmud, Ketubot 110b–111a), according to which banishment from the Land of Israel was divine punishment and the Jewish people had no right to try to force an end to the exile before God made clear that the time had come. For Rabbi Yitzchak Reines (1839–1915), founder of the Mizrachi movement, on the other hand, Zionism was a welcome vehicle for national improvement that had nothing to do with messianism. He supported Zionism as a means to raise the people's dignity and standing and bring them to a happy life. Reines's approach smoothed the path of cooperation with the secular Zionists but disturbed Rav Kook, as it seemed to deny the clearly miraculous, proto-messianic character of the Jewish revival that Zionism had engendered.

---

21 Letter to Rav Ya'akov David Willowsky (The Ridbaz); *Igerot hare'aya* (Jerusalem: Mossad Harav Kook, 2002), 1:348.

His messianic commitments rendered Rav Kook's embrace of Zionism conditional. Jewish nationalism was not a good in itself but was valuable for the values and historical mission that it helped to realize. Kook warned of the danger that nationalism without spiritual content would degenerate into hollow chauvinism. His early Eastern European writings on Zionism bore the imprint of Aḥad Ha'am, for whom ethics was the defining characteristic of the Jewish national spirit.

For the mature Rav Kook, however, the return to the Land of Israel made possible the fulfillment not merely of collective ethics but of holiness, which he understood as that which reveals the unity of things, in all their diversity. In contrast to the classical Jewish understanding of holiness as separateness (e.g., "You shall be holy" [Lev. 19:2] is interpreted by the Sifrei as "you shall be separate"), Rav Kook viewed holiness holistically, as the interrelated harmony of all being. He wrote: "The sacred must be built on the foundation of the profane. The profane is the matter of the sacred, and the sacred is its form; the more powerful the matter, the more significant the form."[22] Holiness is achieved through the integration of the sacred and secular, rather than through their separation. This understanding has its antecedents in the Hasidic idea of *avoda b'gashmiyut*, serving God in the earthly physical world and, before that, in the declaration of the *Tikunei haZohar*, quoted above: "There is no place that is empty of Him."

---

22 *Orot hakodesh* (Jerusalem: Mossad Harav Kook, 1938, 1985), 1:148.

Holiness is present when the spiritual and the material are unified and the connections between them are made manifest. Only through the return of the Jewish people to its own land and the embrace of life in all its dimensions—including, crucially, the aspect of agriculture—could the people's holiness be realized and its spiritual character and mission be articulated. As Rav Kook wrote of the Jewish role in history, "We began to say something of immense importance among ourselves and to the entire world, but we have not yet finished it…. The truth is so rich that we stammer; our speech is still in exile…. In the course of time, we shall be able to express what we seek *with our entire being*."[23]

The most important things in the universe, then, were at stake in the Zionist farmers' struggles to survive by working the land in the Land of Israel. They were gaining a precious physical foothold that would one day lead to the full-fledged flowering of redemption. By returning to agricultural work, they were opening new pathways of holiness, and, as Rav Kook makes clear in the introduction to *Shabbat Ha'aretz*, the unique rhythm of economic life patterned by the laws of *shmita* and *yovel* is a prominent part of the unique message that the Jewish people is called upon to articulate to the world.

Socialism

A strong socialist ethos prevailed among the pioneers of the Second Aliyah, who arrived in Ottoman Palestine in 1904–14

---

23 Quoted in Bokser, *Abraham Isaac Kook*, xix.

and rapidly came to dominate the politics and culture of the Jewish settlement. Many, including Yosef Chaim Brenner and Micha Yosef Berdyczewski, had flirted with revolutionary movements in Russia before emigrating. Immigrants from the Second Aliyah invented the kibbutz, one of the most successful experiments ever in egalitarian communal living.

Many of the central commandments of shmita tend toward creating a more equal society. The requirements that all may come and eat what grows by itself in the fields during the sabbatical year, as well as that loans be forgiven, partially redress the disadvantages of the weak in the marketplace. At a number of places in the introduction to *Shabbat Ha'aretz*, Rav Kook strikes a note of pronounced suspicion about commerce, writing, for example, about "the conflict, compulsion, and pressure … that surround buying, selling, and acquiring things" and our "mundane lives, with their toil, anxiety, anger, and competition."

In his more sustained discussion of socialism, Rav Kook showed a large measure of sympathy with the movement's egalitarian goals, writing: "We do not sorrow if some quality of social justice can be constructed without mention of any spark of the divine because we know that the very aspiration for justice, in whatever form it has, is itself the most illuminating divine influence."[24]

While praising the passion for social justice in socialism, Rav Kook deplored the atheistic, historical materialist philosophy at

---

24 *Igerot hare'aya* 1:45.

the core of Marxism. Yet he was confident that eventually, the atheistic shell of socialism would crumble, revealing the divinely inspired ideals within: "And if man wishes to build the general cosmological structure without any participation of spiritual influence but through calculations of materialistic necessity, we remain serene of heart, observing this child's construction, which builds the shell of life when it does not know how to build life itself, and we draw closer and embrace therefore the connection to life and inner holiness. 'I am the Lord your God who brought you out of the Land of Egypt,' not 'who created the world.'"[25]

Rav Kook reminds us that God's self-identification with the Jewish people at Sinai is not as Creator but as the God who freed slaves from Egypt. Liberation of workers from oppression was a core Jewish spiritual value before Marxist historical materialism.

Particularism and Universalism

The interdependence of particular and universal is a vast theme in Rav Kook's writings; his teachings express a yearning for unity in which all details of life will be integrated into a broad holistic vision. For example: "The more the world develops and becomes whole, the more its parts are united and its organic quality becomes more apparent. The highest unification is the unification of the human's intellect and will with the entire universe, in general and in its particulars."[26]

---

25 Ibid.

26 *Orot hakodesh*, 2:441.

The relationship between the particularity of Israel and the universality of all humanity is a crucial subtheme. Rav Kook's belief in the uniqueness of the people and the Land of Israel is evident throughout the introduction to *Shabbat Ha'aretz*; yet his equally strong universalist commitment is manifest frequently throughout his writings (e.g., "Love for all creatures must live in the heart and soul, love for every individual, and love for all the nations," *Midot hare'aya, ahava* 5). He repeatedly insists that a refined spiritual sensibility must rise above exclusive identification with any one group of people and "sing the song of all creation."

The introduction to *Shabbat Ha'aretz* uses phrases such as "the Jewish people's collective soul" and "this national treasure that is imprinted deep within us," which seem to suggest an essential difference between Jews and others. In fact, Rav Kook's position on this question is quite complex. The nature of the Jewish people's difference from other nations is a classic fault line in Jewish thought, whose key medieval protagonists were Yehuda Halevi and Maimonides. Halevi argues for an inherent, essential difference between Jews and non-Jews.[27] He did not believe that non-Jews could achieve prophecy. Maimonides, on the other hand, argued that the difference of the Jewish people consists in its having received the Torah, a unique manual of ethical training. Maimonides stated in a famous passage[28] that

---

27   E.g., *Kuzari*, 1:27.

28   *Hilkhot shmita v'yovelot* 13:12.

the highest levels of spiritual life are open and accessible to all who are willing to strive for them, Jewish or non-Jewish. In modern times, the Chabad-Lubavitch movement has espoused the essentialist position of Halevi, whereas Rabbi Joseph Dov Soloveitchik, leader of twentieth-century modern orthodoxy, adopted the educational position of Maimonides.

Rav Kook held a harmonistic position synthesizing Maimonides and Halevi; he followed Maimonides' view that individuals of all nations could reach the highest spiritual levels and Halevi's in asserting that the Jewish people possessed an inherent collective uniqueness: "From the perspective of select individuals, we know no distinction between peoples and languages and 'an alien who studies Torah is like a high priest.'… But our extolling of the community of Israel in general is due to the divine quality that is found in the *neshama* of the nation as a whole."[29]

In the introduction to *Shabbat Ha'aretz*, Rav Kook mostly uses the word *neshama* for "soul." This is the highest of three levels of soul that are commonly discussed by the kabbalists: *nefesh*, *ruah*, and *neshama*. Although these three levels are usually applied to the individual, Rav Kook (following other kabbalists, including Rabbi Moshe Chaim Luzzatto)[30] also applied them to collectives and nations. The soul level of *neshama* in individuals is the power of thought and higher will; applied to the collective,

---

29 *Igerot hare'aya* 1:70–71.

30 *Derekh haShem*, part 2, chap. 4.

it represents faith, ethics, religion, the quest for God, and the impulse to charity and justice. Rav Kook asserts here that the Jewish people's collective *neshama* is marked by an especially strong yearning for godliness.

The ultimate goal of Israel's particularism is universal—the perfection of the whole world through the full realization of holiness in the life of the Jewish people.

Halakhah and Aggadah

A notable aspect of Rav Kook's quest to reveal the unity of all creation and phenomena was his passion to reconnect halakhah and aggadah. The Talmud is made up of roughly equal quantities of halakhic, legal discussion, and aggadic material, comprising stories, folklore, fantastic tales, midrashic retellings of the lives of biblical figures, philosophical reflection, ethical meditations, astronomical and other scientific observations, medical remedies, recipes, and much more. These divergent types of writing are thoroughly interwoven throughout the Talmud. Despite the editorial mixing of the two media, halakhah and aggadah are generally treated separately; indeed, in traditional yeshivot, aggadah is not usually treated at all but is skipped over as a distraction.

Rav Kook regretted this omission and called for a reintegration of the halakhah with the aggadah.[31] In his thinking, the halakhah and aggadah are frequently reflecting on common themes but

---

31   *Orot hakodesh*, 1:25.

in different cognitive modes. For example, the Talmud will shift from one register to another when the spiritual principle underlying a legal dispute calls forth a story as an illustration of its emotional depths. For him, the prevalent sense of separation between the two realms "removes the primary content of spiritual creativity; the tranquillity that comes from inner unity."[32] In Rav Kook's view, to cut off norm from narrative, logic from imagination, rigor from reality, is to sever the unity of the mind and risk disturbing the creativity that flourishes through the free flow of ideas between different modes of thought.

The same idea was expressed lyrically by a contemporary of Rav Kook's, the poet Chaim Nachman Bialik, who wrote: "Halakhah and aggadah are two things that are really one: two sides of a single shield.... Halakhah is the crystallization, the ultimate and inevitable quintessence of aggadah; aggadah is the content of halakhah. Aggadah is the plaintive voice of the heart's yearning as it wings its way to its haven; halakhah is the resting place, where, for a moment, the yearning is satisfied and stilled. As a dream seeks its fulfillment in interpretation, as will in action, as thought in speech, as flower in fruit—so halakhah in aggadah."[33]

The relationship between the introduction to *Shabbat Ha'aretz* and the main body of the book is an example of this

---

32 Ibid.

33 Chaim Nahman Bialik, "Halachah and Aggadah," in *Revealment and Concealment: Five Essays*, trans. Leon Simon (Jerusalem: Ibis, 2000), 46.

project of integration. The main text of *Shabbat Ha'aretz* is a 120-page halakhic argument in favor of the *heter mekhira* leniency that permitted selling parts of the Land of Israel to non-Jews in the shmita year so as to avoid observing many of the stringent shmita laws. As well as arguing for the *heter*, however, Rav Kook endeavored to educate about the importance of shmita. This was the purpose of the non-halakhic introduction to *Shabbat Ha'aretz*, translated here, which discusses the socioeconomic, philosophical, and mystical significance of shmita.

The Argument of *Shabbat Ha'aretz*

The halakhic content of *Shabbat Ha'aretz* was bold and innovative. Indeed, one of the book's novel features was that it was explicitly innovative. Rav Kook was not content to present the *heter mekhira* as a seamless evolution of Jewish law; unusually for a halakhic innovator, he stressed that he was proposing something new, arguing that the resettlement of the Land of Israel was a sufficiently radical development to require novel halakhic treatment:

> *The sabbatical dispensation by a permit of sale on which we rely was never used and does not appear to have been relied upon by the early sages, of blessed memory, at the time of the Second Temple, in all the days of the sages of the Jerusalem Talmud, nor when the population continued to live in the Land of Israel afterward…. This is not surprising; in the early generations, the need was not so pressing…. Whenever there was no pressing need, the*

sages did not want to publicize dispensations based on legal fiction, following the maxim "It is the glory of the Lord to conceal a matter" (Prov. 25:2).... In the early days, when Jews lived primarily by working the land for sustenance, it was possible to observe the sanctity of the sabbatical year according to the details of the law without any dispensation; but in our days, when the existence of the community depends on commerce in the produce and crops of the agricultural settlements and the effect of preventing commerce would also lead to the destruction of future stability—under these circumstances, it is certainly our obligation to introduce the dispensation by way of sale of the land.[34]

Rav Kook alludes to the discretion with which halakhic authorities usually introduce innovation ("It is the glory of the Lord to conceal a matter"). This approach would not do in the present case, he argued. In the new situation—where the community subsisted by commerce in agricultural produce, including for export—it was imperative to introduce the dispensation of selling the land, and to do so publicly, to demonstrate the halakhah's responsiveness to the changed reality.

Rav Kook addressed four basic issues in his argument for the *heter*: (1) whether the sabbatical year is a rabbinic prohibition (rather than a biblical prohibition) in contemporary times; (2)

---

34 *Shabbat Ha'aretz*, 59–61.

whether non-Jewish acquisition of land in the Land of Israel suspends its sanctity; (3) whether it is, in fact, permissible to sell land in the Land of Israel to a non-Jew; and (4) whether such a fictional sale has enough validity to actually effect the suspension of the sanctity of the land.

Is Shmita a Rabbinic or Torah Prohibition in Our Times?

In order to set aside shmita by selling the land, it was essential for Rav Kook to establish that shmita in post-Temple times is of weaker rabbinic authority (*miderabanan*) rather than having the force of a Torah law (*mide'oraita*). This question had been extensively debated over centuries, and there were three major opinions:

1. Shmita today has the force of a Torah law; Rabbi Yosef Karo, author of the *Shulḥan arukh*, maintained that this was the opinion of Maimonides[35] (although Maimonides' text clearly allows for the opposite interpretation).

2. Shmita today has the force of a rabbinic law. This was the most widely held opinion.[36] There were two main reasons given in the talmudic sources as to why this should be so. The first, attributed to Rabbi Yehuda Hanasi, was that shmita and *yovel*, the Jubilee year, were

---

35 Based on a reading of Maimonides, *Mishne Torah, Hilkhot shmita v'yovel* 10:9.

36 See, e.g., Tur, *Yoreh De'ah* 331; Ritva, Rashba, and *Sefer haḥinukh* also held this opinion.

intimately connected. Jubilee is longer observed, so the shmita cannot be fully observed, either: "When the Jubilee was in operation, shmita was in practice on the authority of the Torah; now that the Jubilee is not in operation, shmita is practiced as a rabbinic ordinance."[37] The Jubilee is practiced, according to the Talmud, "when all the land's inhabitants are living there." Its practice ceased during the First Temple period, when two and a half of the tribes were exiled.[38] The other reason is that the agricultural laws in general are not in force during the post-Temple period.

3. Shmita today does not even have rabbinic force but is a *midat ḥasidut* (supra-legal standard of piety). This was the view of the Provençal scholars Rabbi Zeraḥaya Halevi[39] (Razah) and Rabbi Avraham David of Posquières (Ravad).

Having reviewed the extensive halakhic sources and argued compellingly that (2) was correct, Rav Kook asked an interesting question: If the obligation to observe shmita does not have the force of a Torah law, why did the rabbis establish it as even a rabbinic obligation? His striking answer is that the rabbis

---

37 Talmud Yerushalmi, Shevi'it 10:2.

38 Ibid.; Talmud Bavli, Arakhin 32b.

39 The opinion of Razah is cited by *Sefer haterumot*, 55:4; Meiri, *Sefer magen avot*, 15. Recently, it was taken up and adopted by the Conservative halakhic writer Rabbi David Golinkin.

instituted it as a memorial of the full shmita: "Its performance is primarily as a remembrance."[40] Keeping shmita in our times is, among other things, an educational tool for keeping alive the ideal of what it could and should one day be. This leads Rav Kook to the remarkable idea that these educational goals can also be accomplished by marking one's avoidance of shmita observance—for example, through the *heter mekhira*: "Since the evasion is carried out according to the prescriptions of the law, it constitutes a remembrance of the precept so that the law will not be forgotten, and when the time comes again for them to observe the biblical law, all the laws will be known."[41] Through the *heter mekhira*, shmita is more honored in the breach than the observance.

Does Non-Jewish Acquisition of the Land Suspend Its Sanctity?

The question of whether selling the land to non-Jews does, in fact, suspend the holiness of the land was debated in sixteenth-century Tzfat by Rabbi Yosef Karo and Rabbi Moshe de Trani. Rav Kook followed Karo's view that it indeed does;[42] Karo argued, in effect, that the sanctity of the land as applied to

---

40 *Shabbat Ha'aretz*, 59. This is reminiscent of the midrash from Sifrei Deuteronomy, which taught that the reason for observing the commandments in exile was as reminders or "as road markers," an idea that was adopted by Naḥmanides in his Torah commentary.

41 Ibid.

42 Rabbi Yosef Karo, *Responsa Avkat Rokhel*, §§22–25.

the agricultural commandments is not an absolute, objective category but a normative one and applies, as do most of the other commandments, to Jews. Rav Kook combined this view with the opinion that shmita today is rabbinic and concluded that the rabbinic level of sabbatical-year sanctity in modern times would be suspended by the sale of the land to a non-Jew.

The Ridbaz and others pointed out the paradox that, out of a commitment to the settling of the Land of Israel and a deep conviction of its sanctity, Rav Kook was willing to suspend that sanctity by selling it to non-Jews. Rav Kook responded by distinguishing among various kinds and levels of holiness: "In situations where the biblical level of sanctity remains, the acquisition of land by a non-Jew does not suspend its sanctity; but when the level of sanctity is rabbinic, it is suspended by sale to a non-Jew."[43] He argued that there is a holiness to the Land of Israel and an intrinsic merit in living there that does not depend on the fulfillment of the commandments and therefore persists even if it is impossible, for whatever reason, to fulfill certain commandments: "[The sages] said, 'Settling in the Land of Israel is equal to all the other commandments of the Torah.' This means that settling there in itself is the [manifestation of the] primary sanctity of the Land of Israel. The merit of the agricultural commandments relating to the land are drawn along with it as a result. Yet even when [the precepts relating to the land] are suspended because of an urgent situation, [the primary sanctity]

---

43 *Shabbat Ha'aretz*, 45.

remains intact."[44]

May One Sell the Land of Israel to Non-Jews?

The biblical prohibition of *lo teḥoneim* (Deut. 7:1–2) was divided by the rabbis into three prohibitions[45]—one of them being interpreted to mean that you shall not give them (i.e., idolaters) a foothold in the land. This was widely understood as a prohibition against selling the land to non-Jews and was therefore an obstacle to the *heter mekhira*.

Rav Kook marshaled a number of arguments against this objection. He argued that prohibiting the *heter mekhira* on the basis of *lo teḥoneim* would be entirely self-defeating. Surely, the purpose of the law in Deuteronomy was to promote Jewish ownership of the Land of Israel, whereas literal observance of shmita without the *heter* would cause Jews to have to leave their land and possibly return to Europe. Maintaining the underlying principle of the law required making an exception. Moreover, he argued, one could rely on the opinion of the great medieval scholar Rabbi Menachem haMeiri (1249–1315) that non-Jews who follow monotheistic religions are not to be considered idolaters. Meiri defined a new halakhic category, *umot hagedurot bedat*, nations that were bound by a religion and that therefore, unlike idolaters, subscribe to moral norms. Meiri took Christians and Muslims of his day to fall into this category; consequently,

---

44 Ibid., 62–63.

45 Talmud Bavli, Avoda Zara 20a.

they were exempt from restrictions that the halakhah had applied to lawless idol worshipers. For those unwilling to rely on Meiri, Rav Kook argued that one could employ the widely held opinion of Maimonides that Muslims were not idolaters and that therefore the prohibition on selling land in Israel did not apply to them.[46]

Are Legal Fictions Justified?

Rav Kook was seriously exercised by the questions of whether legal fictions in general were justified in Jewish law and, if so, whether a fictitious sale was effective in a case where the clear intent of the parties was to evade a law and not to effect a lasting transfer of ownership. The issue is complicated; suffice it to say that Rav Kook concluded that the use of legal fictions was justified. "The Jerusalem Talmud states that to be merciful with the property of Israel, it is permissible to evade [the law]. And where there is great necessity, as seems to be the case regarding the question of the sabbatical laws, in view of the current situation, it is proper, according to this [principle], to rule leniently."[47] The crucial question for Rav Kook was, what are the values and principles for the sake of which it is warranted to employ legal fictions?

---

46 Maimonides, *Mishne Torah, Hilkhot Avoda Zara* 10:6.

47 Talmud Yerushalmi, Beitza 3:2; *Shabbat Ha'aretz*, 57.

Meta-Halakhic Principles of Shabbat Ha'aretz

Shabbat Ha'aretz became a defining piece of Religious Zionist *psak halakhah* (halakhic decision making) and has served as a lightning rod for controversy between Religious Zionists and ḥaredim about the proper parameters of halakhic innovation in Israel. It owes this status to Rav Kook's openness about the meta-halakhic principles that motivated and justified his embrace of the *heter*. These principles revolve around a recognition of the *national* dimensions of the return to Israel. Halakhah in Israel, he believed, must strive to find solutions for the collective rather than being content to regulate the lives of observant individuals or subsectors.[48]

First, Rav Kook explicitly invoked the value of enabling Jews to live and flourish economically in the Land of Israel as a justification for the *heter*: "What would we say in a situation that affects the *nation as a whole* in reference to the settlement of the Jews in their land? Would not everyone certainly agree that it is permissible to rely on a lone opinion in matters that are rabbinic by nature?"[49]

Second, he asserted that the Land of Israel was the national center of the whole Jewish people. Believing that concerns about shmita were deterring religious Jews from immigrating,

---

48 Arye Edrei, "From Orthodoxy to Religious Zionism: Rabbi Kook and the Sabbatical Year Polemic," trans. Shmuel Peerless, http://www2.tau.ac.il/InternetFiles/news/UserFiles//Shmita.pdf (2008), 107–9.

49 *Mishpat Kohen* (Jerusalem: Mossad Harav Kook, 1966), 63.

he felt responsible to find a solution that would enable these Jews to move to the Land of Israel with confidence that shmita observance would not destroy their livelihood.[50]

Third, as Arye Edrei convincingly shows, Rav Kook was concerned with expanding the target audience for his halakhic decisions from the religiously observant of the Old Yishuv to all Jews living in the Land of Israel, whether observant or not. When the Ridbaz suggested to Rav Kook that they solve the shmita issue by going to Europe to raise money to support religious farmers who wished to cease work in the shmita, Kook responded that this was a solution for small numbers but not for the majority.[51] He felt responsible to make the halakhah work—at least as a potential option—for the whole Yishuv, even those who currently identified as outsiders to the observant community.

The Introduction to *Shabbat Ha'aretz*: The Aggadah of Shmita

Shabbat Ha'aretz is a rigorous and detailed halakhic treatment of what was and was not to be done in the shmita of 1909–10 and why. Characteristically, Rav Kook prefaced the book with an introduction written in an entirely different register. These pages are a poetic and mystical paean to the possibilities of shmita. Their principal point of connection to the halakhic work is in

---

50   Ibid.

51   Edrei, "From Orthodoxy to Religious Zionism," 100.

Rav Kook's argument, briefly discussed above, that the talmudic sages enjoined the continued observance of shmita as a reminder of what it could one day be. The introduction is an ecstatic effort to render the reminder as vividly as possible.

In this prefatory section, Rav Kook paints a picture of shmita as enabling a renewed connection to the divine life force in each individual and within us collectively. Like Sabbath, shmita quiets the tumult of the intervening periods and restores a more authentic relationship to ourselves, to one another, to nature, and to God. Its observance reveals the unique weave of socioeconomic relationships that the Torah would have us pattern. The Jubilee year is a revelation of the cumulative insight and holiness that we will have achieved in the previous seven shmita cycles. Its ideals of liberty and emancipation bear universal meanings for the whole of humanity. Rav Kook outlines a biblically based schema of Jewish history in which our ancestors' avaricious neglect of shmita led to exile from the Land of Israel and a prolonged divorce from the earthly, physical dimensions of life. This lengthy period of ethereal existence refined the people's ethical sensibility, and they began once more to long for a return to their homeland. Rav Kook hoped that this nascent resettlement of the land would lead one day to the mitzvot connected to the land, shmita foremost among them, being observed in all their glory. Yet he realized that the state of the agricultural pioneers was still precarious and that most would need to avail themselves of the *heter mekhira*, so that the Yishuv could continue to grow and flourish to the point where full shmita observance would eventually be possible. Meanwhile, he urged his readers to continue to study all they could about shmita, as learning led to action and would help bring closer the day when shmita would be observed in Israel as it should be.

But how *should* it ideally be observed? Clearly, Rav Kook hoped that one day it would be possible for all the halakhot of shmita to be operational, including observance of the prohibitions against doing most forms of agricultural labor. But he envisioned much more: a periodic outbreak of justice, equality, psychic rebirth, and restored universal human dignity amounting to a comprehensive spiritual and social renewal. How does Rav Kook help us to understand what that would look like or how to go about getting there?

Although Rav Kook's prose in the introduction is lyrical and rather short on specifics, there are a number of places where he provides us with striking images of what the ideal *shmita* or Jubilee might be like. These can provide highly suggestive and stimulating guideposts. Some of them point along lines that contemporary thinkers and activists are already pursuing; others are arrestingly original. I will briefly discuss seven of them.

1. Shmita is for the community what Sabbath is for the individual.

"What Sabbath does for the individual, shmita does for the nation as a whole," writes Rav Kook in the introduction. "Just as it was said about the Sabbath of Creation, 'It is a Sabbath for God,' so, too, it was said about the Sabbath of shmita: 'It is a Sabbath for God.'" Shmita, like Sabbath, is envisaged as a time for us all to step out of the nonstop scramble of getting and spending and to renew ourselves, restoring our connection with the unique, divine life that flows in each one of us. What might this mean today? Daniel Taub, now Israel's ambassador to London, beautifully expressed the possibilities of a universal sabbatical in an essay that he wrote two *shmitot* ago:

> [Shmita is a] time to see ourselves not in terms of what we do, but what we are, and even what we might become.... For any of us, to learn that instrument, to write that book, to try the path we never took.... The cost—decommissioning a seventh of the productive workforce—might sound steep. But it is an investment with potentially exponential rewards. For the workplace: a continuous stream of invigorated employees, brimming with insights and experiences; for families: a time for reacquaintance and renewal; for society: an opportunity for caring individuals to devote not just the margins of their weeks but the very kernels of their days to the underprivileged; for culture: an invitation to untapped masses to learn to appreciate, to explore, and to create; for our youth: a promise that passion and opportunity will not be buried forever with their first paycheck; and, perhaps most of all, for our seniors: a chance to prepare for the increasingly traumatic transition

to retirement and to preempt the dread "if only" that threatens to haunt our final years.[52]

2. Shmita is an expression of the interconnection between people and land.

Rav Kook views shmita as an outstanding instance of the inextricable connection between the people and the Land of Israel. Both embody an innate rhythm that longs for and requires relief and renewal once every seven years. As Rav Kook puts it in the introduction to *Shabbat Ha'aretz*:

> *The distinctive character of the people and the land dovetail with each other. Just as the people has a special aptitude for reaching spiritual heights from within the depths of everyday life, so, too, the land—God's land—forms the people who dwell there as an everlasting inheritance that comes through a covenant and promise, with faith in the Eternal One of Israel, and is founded on the divine nature immovably infused in this wonderful country, which is married to the people whom God chose. The soul of the people and the land intertwine, working from the basis of their being to bring into existence the intricate patterns of inner holiness that lie within them during the sabbatical year. The people works with its soul force on the land, and*

---

52 Daniel Taub, "Scratching the Seven-Year Itch" (unpublished essay, 2000).

> *the land works on the people, refining their character in line*
> *with the divine desire for life inherent in their makeup.*
> *The people and the land both need a year of Sabbath!*

How should we read such passages today, when metaphysical assertions of the indissoluble connection between the Jewish people and the Land of Israel tend to accompany certain particular political claims—for example, to Israeli sovereignty over the biblical heartlands of Judaea and Samaria? Can readers who are not inclined to accept such claims stretch their sympathies toward an understanding of Rav Kook's underlying idea?

Rav Kook's sensibility and meaning in speaking of the connection between people and land were much closer, I would suggest, to that of the great American prophet of agrarianism, Wendell Berry, than to Gush Emunim. The land for Rav Kook was not primarily important as an abstraction. He wrote and, apparently, thought little about land as a political category. He was patently thrilled by participating in the Jewish people's reacquaintance with the earthy facts of its ancestral homeland. Whether kissing stones, crying as he placed a sapling tree into the soil, or gleefully traveling in a dirty hay cart when he visited the settlement of Merhavia, Rav Kook rejoiced in the reality of knowing, seeing, and touching the particular places that had been formative of the Jewish people's spiritual character. His enthusiasm for the pioneering farmers and laments about the impoverished character of a Diaspora Judaism that had been exiled from the soil are reminiscent of Wendell Berry's complaints about a Christianity that had become cut off from physical, biological reality; or, as Berry put it: "my own long held belief that Christianity, as usually presented by its organizations, is not *earthly* enough—that valid spiritual life, in this world, must have a practice and a practicality—it must have a material result."[53] (Or, as he puts it more pithily, "I don't think it is appreciated how much of an outdoor book the Bible is.")[54]

A consciousness of the interwovenness of the Land of Israel with the Jewish people and its history, culture, and religion pervades the introduction to *Shabbat Ha'aretz*. It should not, I would contend, be read through the prism of political developments that occurred long after Rav Kook's death; rather, it is a call to recover the awareness that Berry writes of when he says:

> *We have given up the understanding—dropped it out of our language and so out of our thought—that we and our country create one another, depend on one another, are literally part of one another; that our land passes in and out of our bodies just as our bodies pass in and out of our land; that as we and our land are part of one another, so all who are living as neighbors here, human and plant*

53 Wendell Berry, "The Gift of Good Land," in *The Gift of Good Land: Further Essays Cultural and Agricultural* (Berkeley, Calif.: Counterpoint, 1981), 267.
54 Idem, *The Art of the Commonplace: The Agrarian Essays* (Berkeley, Calif.: Counterpoint, 2003).

and animal, are part of one another, and so cannot possibly flourish alone; that, therefore, our culture must be our response to our place, our culture and our place are images of each other and inseparable from each other, and so neither can be better than the other.[55]

3. In the shmita, treat food as food, not as a commodity.

Claims to private property will not profane the holiness of the produce of the land during this year, and the urge to get rich, which is stimulated by trade, will be forgotten; as it says, "for you to eat—but not for your trade."

Rav Kook emphasizes the principle, rooted in a number of halakhot of shmita, that in that year, food is for eating, not for trading. The biblical verse says, "The sabbatical produce shall be for you *to eat*" (Lev. 25:6), based on which uses of the produce, other than directly eating it, are restricted. As Maimonides codified it in his *Mishne Torah*: "We may not use the produce of the sabbatical year for commercial activity. If one desires to sell a small amount of the produce of the sabbatical year, he may.... He should use it only to purchase food and eat that food according to the restrictions of the holiness of the sabbatical year."[56] In the sabbatical year, produce grown in Israel becomes sanctified. Its

---

55 Idem, *The Unsettling of America* (San Francisco: Sierra Club, 1977).

56 Maimonides, *Mishne Torah*, Seder Zera'im, *Hilkhot shmita v'yovel* 6:1.

holiness is honored when we eat it as food but desecrated if we use it for profit through trading the food as a commodity.

The global food business today is worth billions of dollars, and it is treated as an industry like any other. The industrialization of agriculture has enabled the mass production of cheap food that has fed millions, especially in the Third World, but has also come with serious costs. This shmita principle challenges us to return to a more natural and immediate relationship to the food we eat—for example, by eating more *food* rather than food-like products manufactured from dozens of artificially synthesized ingredients.[57]

4. Shmita as a year of human health

> *Human beings will return to a state of natural health, so that they will not need healing for sicknesses, which mostly befall us when the balance of life is destroyed and our lives are distanced from the rhythms of nature; "for you to eat" but not to make medicine and not to use as bandages.*

Rav Kook here makes the astonishing claim that in the shmita, people will naturally return to a state of physical health. He bases this on the halakhah that in the shmita, food products should not be used to make bandages, poultices, and other medicinal

---

57 Michael Pollan makes this provocative distinction in *In Defense of Food* (New York: Penguin, 2008).

products. (This is also based on Lev. 25:6, which teaches that you should the produce of shmita "as food"—but not, the rabbis infer, as medicine).[58] Rav Kook suggests that such things simply will not be necessary in the ideal shmita; health will flow from a restoration of natural equilibrium.

Only the most extreme natural-health fanatic would take such a claim at face value, rather than as hyperbole or messianic dreaming. Conversely, only the narrowest adherents of a mechanistic, biomedical approach to health and illness could fail to be struck by Rav Kook's insight that lifestyle imbalance tends to cause disease (or dis-ease, as holistic health practitioners prefer to write it). Decades before the development of the medical research field of psycho-neuro-immunology, which demonstrated that prolonged stress suppresses the immune system and is a causative factor in a spectrum of diseases ranging from heart disease to depression, Rav Kook points out that ceaseless activity is bad for us and that the rest and renewal that shmita offers can promote health and healing.

5. Shmita and the Jubilee are interconnected rhythms and structures.

> *Holiness grows throughout these spans of time: "Count the shmita years in order to sanctify the Jubilees,"[59] to prepare*

---

58 Talmud, Sukkah 40b, Mishnah Shevi'it 8:1.

59 Talmud Bavli, Arakhin 32b.

life for the Jubilee. "And you shall count off seven weeks of
seven years—seven times seven years—so that the period
of seven weeks of seven years gives you a total of forty-nine
years."[60]

Insight and consciousness build over each shmita cycle, until a kind of culmination at the end of seven cycles, with the Jubilee and an outbreak of universal freedom and emancipation. Rav Kook sees the Jubilee and shmita cycles as intimately connected. This chimes with his halakhic position (outlined above) that since Jubilee and shmita are interdependent and the Jubilee is not operative in our times, shmita today is only a rabbinic obligation.

Shmita observance is cumulative. Rav Kook emphasized that this cumulative characteristic of shmita results from our moral choices to deepen and broaden the implementation of the values and practices of shmita. He believed that whereas the impulse and need to observe shmita is innate, the potential of shmita to grow and evolve with each round of observance depends on how we choose to practice it. The implication of this insight is that renewed interest in shmita and experimentation around its public forms should grow and deepen, cycle by cycle. Through each iteration, our understanding of the possibilities of shmita may grow into new structures of observance and consciousness that we cannot currently imagine.

---

60 Lev. 25:8.

6. Jubilee as a year of truth and reconciliation

> *The spirit of the Jubilee will gather great strength, until it has sufficient potency not only to reveal the goodness within the soul of the people, ... as does the shmita, but also to fix the crookedness and brokenness of the past.... "Then you shall sound the horn loud; in the seventh month on the tenth day of the month—the Day of Atonement—you shall have the horn sounded throughout your land,"[61] and a godly spirit of general forgiveness, such as the individual experiences on Yom Kippur—will arise through the holiness of the Jubilee.... From Rosh Hashanah until Yom Kippur, slaves would neither become free to go home, nor would they remain slaves to their masters, but they would eat, drink, and rejoice with crowns on their heads. When Yom Kippur would arrive, the beit din would sound the shofar, slaves would be free to go home, and fields would return to their original owners.[62]*

The Jubilee was a time when slaves went free and land returned to its ancestral owners. Whatever inequalities had accumulated in the previous forty-nine years, the Jubilee restored each to his original dignity. Rav Kook gives a beautiful reading of a talmudic passage that fills in the interpersonal dimension of this economic

---

61   Lev. 25:9.

62   Talmud, Rosh Hashanah 8b.

drama. The Talmud points out a contradiction between the Mishnah (Rosh Hashanah 1:1), which says that the first day of Tishrei—Rosh Hashanah—is the start of the Jubilee, and the verse in Leviticus 25 that says that the shofar blast marking the start of the Jubilee and the freeing of slaves was sounded on the tenth of Tishrei—Yom Kippur. When did the Jubilee start, and when were slaves actually freed? By way of resolution, the Talmud quotes the opinion that slaves were freed from servitude on Rosh Hashanah but only free to go home after the shofar blast on Yom Kippur. In the interim, they ate, drank, and celebrated with their former masters.

By quoting this in the context of the view of the Jubilee as a year of forgiveness that "rectifies the injustices of the past," Rav Kook frames the scene of the slaves feasting on an equal footing with their erstwhile owners during their final days together as integral to that process of forgiveness. The Torah also requires the master to send off his servants with gifts. These leveling acts help heal the social scars and psychological wounds caused by economic divisions and class estrangement. Rav Kook recognizes that national healing requires not just freeing the slaves; the indignity and humiliation that they endured over many years must also be addressed and overcome. One wonders whether he foresaw the failures of revolutionary movements that treated economic emancipation as a sufficient goal and ended up merely switching out the ruling class while perpetuating oppression and cruelty.

7. Jubilee as a universal principle

> Such life-affirming flights of possibility [in the Jubilee
> year] will raise up the people to bind its life together with
> all humanity through those special people, the gerim
> toshavim—*non-Jews who … feel a special connection
> to the reinvigorated spiritual aspirations of the Jewish
> people.… "The law of a Hebrew servant and the law of
> the* ger toshav *operate only when the Jubilee operates."*[63]

Rav Kook intuited that there is a strong universal dimension to the
idea of the Jubilee. He inferred this from the talmudic statement
that the institution of *ger toshav* is only operational in an era
when the Jubilee is in force. *Ger toshav* is a status for non-Jews
who feel drawn to the Jewish people and take upon themselves
to observe the seven Noahide laws in the Land of Israel. Rav
Kook understood there to be an inner connection between the
two concepts; the *gerim toshavim* would be the channel through
which the ideals of the Jubilee reach all humanity.

Neither the laws of Jubilee nor of *ger toshav* operate today,
and it is unclear whether or how either will ever be reinstated.
Nevertheless, Rav Kook's sense of the universal appeal of the
Jubilee ideal was clearly correct. Other Jewish thinkers have also
seen in the Jubilee economic thought that could apply beyond
the boundaries of the Jewish people. Rabbi Samson Raphael

---

63 Talmud, Arakhin 29a.

Hirsch advocated the Jubilee as a universal antidote to economic inequality in his Bible commentary; in 1930, the Revisionist Zionist thinker Ze'ev Jabotinsky wrote an important essay arguing that the biblical Jubilee idea should be the blueprint for the future economic system because it avoided both the suffocating control of socialism and the obscene inequalities of unbridled capitalism.[64]

Early American thinkers repeatedly invoked the Jubilee to express the universality of freedom. In 1751, when the Pennsylvania Assembly ordered a special bell to be cast, commemorating the fiftieth anniversary of William Penn's Charter of Privileges, the Speaker of the Assembly was entrusted with finding an appropriate inscription to express the charter's aspirations to freedom and equality. What later became the Liberty Bell inscription was taken from the biblical verse describing the Jubilee year: "Proclaim Liberty thro' all the Land to all the Inhabitants thereof" (Lev. 25:10). The Jubilee idea inspired the United States Homestead Act of 1862, which parceled out land holdings to small farmers. The influential nineteenth-century American economist Henry George took the Jubilee idea as the inspiration for the theory that there should be a single tax on land to prevent land speculation, which George saw as the main cause of entrenched economic inequality. (The

---

64 Samson Raphael Hirsch, *The Hirsch Chumash* (New York: Feldheim, 2009); and Ze'ev Jabotinsky, "The Jubilee Ideal," in idem, *Nation and Society* (Tel Aviv: Beitar, 1961), 62–67.

game of Monopoly was invented by a follower of George as an educational tool to demonstrate the evil effects of rent in impoverishing tenants and enriching landlords.)

More recently, the Jubilee 2000 movement took the Jubilee as the inspiration for its demand that $90 billion of Third World loans be forgiven so as to lift the crippling effects of historical debt and give dozens of developing countries a new chance to grow and flourish. In the aftermath of the 2007–9 crash, in which debt and economic inequality were both centrally implicated, Jubilee thinking has resurfaced once again. It is safe to assume that the Jubilee concept has not exhausted its potential as a universal source of inspiration for radical economic reform.

Conclusion: The Text

Rav Kook's introduction to *Shabbat Ha'aretz* is a difficult and opaque text. It combines lyrical poetry, kabbalistic speculation, sweeping (though often also profound) schematizations of Jewish history, reflections on the socioeconomic possibilities of shmita, and a justification for the halakhic work that follows. As in most of his writings, here, too, Rav Kook quotes biblical, talmudic, and kabbalistic sources, mostly without attribution. Sometimes he rereads these sources in brilliant and insightful ways, creatively recasting them as resources for his argument.

The introduction panoramically scans Jewish history 2,500 years into the past, but its vision primarily focuses on the future. Rav Kook gazes forward to a fuller and richer realization of shmita than was possible in the precarious economic circumstances of his time and place. His vision is, on occasion, blurry, and sometimes reality merges into the messianic horizon. Yet here and there, we can discern contours of a future that, with the benefit of being a century closer to it than Rav Kook, we might also recognize as possible.

NOTE ON THE TRANSLATION

Translating Rav Kook's writings is a challenging privilege. The privilege lies in the immense profundity, beauty, and importance of his writings; it is a joy to make them more widely available to the English-speaking world. Among the challenges: his sentences are often very long; the syntax can be confusing; the style and vocabulary are influenced by a genre of nineteenth-century belles lettres that is long out of fashion; the subject matter is frequently esoteric or mystical; he quotes from the whole repertoire of traditional Jewish sources, usually without attribution; and occasionally, the thought that he is expressing remains elusive even after repeated rereading of a sentence or passage.

In his classic essay on English style, "Politics and the English Language," George Orwell gives six rules for writing. Number six is "break any of these rules sooner than say anything outright barbarous." I have strained to convey Rav Kook's meaning while staying as close as possible to his syntax, sentence structure, and word choice. Occasionally, however, I saw no alternative but to break the rules in order to render Rav Kook's thought in non-barbarous English.

שַׁבַּת הָאָרֶץ
הִלְכוֹת שְׁבִיעִית

מֵאֵת הָרַב ר' אַבְרָהָם יִצְחָק הַכֹּהֵן קוּק זצ"ל

ה ַק ָד ָמ ה

רָאשֵׁי-פְּרָקִים עַל עֵרֶךְ הַשְּׁמִטָּה וְהַיּוֹבֵל בְּחַיֵּי יִשְׂרָאֵל בִּכְלָל
וּבְתֶחִיַּת הָאֻמָּה, הָאָרֶץ וְהַתּוֹרָה, בְּאוֹר ד', חַי הָעוֹלָמִים

Shabbat Ha'aretz, Introduction

Rabbi Abraham Isaac Kook

A summary of the value of shmita and yovel in the life of the Jewish people generally and in the revival of the nation, the life, and the Torah, in the light of God, Life of the World

וּמִי כְעַמְּךָ כְּיִשְׂרָאֵל גּוֹי אֶחָד בָּאָרֶץ (שמואל ב', ז' כ"ג) גּוֹי אֶחָד בָּאָרֶץ,
וַדַּאי בָּאָרֶץ הֵם גּוֹי אֶחָד, עַמָּה אִקְרוּן אֶחָד וְלֹא אִינּוּן בִּלְחוֹדַיְיהוּ.

(זהר ויקרא צ"ג ב')

הַשְּׁמִטָּה וְהַיּוֹבֵל בַּוְּמַנִּים, מִתְיַחֲסִים זֶה לָזֶה, כְּמוֹ הַחַמָּה וְהַלְּבָנָה
בָּעוֹלָם וּכְמוֹ יִשְׂרָאֵל וְהָאָדָם בְּנַפְשׁוֹת, - יַחַס הַפְּרָט וְהַכְּלָל, שֶׁהֵם,
בְּמוּבָנָם הָעַצְמִי הַיּוֹתֵר חַי וְיוֹתֵר רוּחָנִי, צְרִיכִים זֶה לָזֶה: פְּרָט
הַצָּרִיךְ לַכְּלָל וּכְלָל הַצָּרִיךְ לַפְּרָט.

1. In choosing this quotation from the Zohar, the classic work of Jewish mysti-
    cism, as the epigram for his book about shmita, Rav Kook suggests that the
    uniqueness of the Jewish people is fully manifested only when they are living
    on their land and practicing the laws that regulate life in harmony with the
    earth—shmita foremost among them.

2. In Leviticus 25, the primary biblical source for shmita, the sabbatical and
    Jubilee years are interconnected parts of a fifty-year cycle; see Lev. 25:2–10.

Who is like Your people Israel, a unique nation on earth?
(2 Sam. 7:23)

"Who is like your people Israel, a unique nation on earth?"
When they are united with the land, they are called a unique
nation, but not when they are separate from it.
(Zohar, Leviticus 93b)[1]

The sabbatical and Jubilee years are interconnected in
time,[2] like the sun and the moon in the universe, like
Israel and humanity in the world of souls.[3] The particular
and the universal are profoundly interdependent in the
most vital and spiritual sense; the particular needs the
universal, and the universal needs the particular.[4]

3. Rav Kook alludes here to the foundational kabbalistic notion of *ashan*, an
    acronym of *olam, shana, nefesh*, or world, time, and soul, the three dimensions
    that shape the finite world. The concept of *ashan* first appears in *Sefer Yet-*
    zirah, the oldest extant work of Jewish mysticism, references to which occur
    in texts from the first century (see *Sefer Yetzirah* 4:7–4:14, trans. Aryeh Ka-
    plan [York Beach, Me.: Samuel Weiser, 1990]). Rav Kook's otherwise rather
    enigmatic reference to the sun and moon as instances of the particular and
    the universal appears to refer back to *Sefer Yetzirah* 4:7. See *Orot hakodesh*
    (Jerusalem: Mossad Harav Kook, 1938, 1985), 2:313, for an expanded expla-
    nation of Rav Kook's understanding of the holiness inherent in these three
    basic dimensions of existence.

4. The interdependence of the particular and the universal is a major theme in
    Rav Kook's writings. For an especially penetrating discussion of the relation-
    ship between these poles of Rav Kook's thought, see Yehudah Mirsky, *Rav*
    Kook: Mystic in a Time of Revolution (New Haven, Conn.: Yale University
    Press, 2014), 107–11. See also the introduction to this volume, p. 51.

"מִי גוֹי גָדוֹל אֲשֶׁר לוֹ אֱלֹהִים קְרֹבִים אֵלָיו!" – סְגֻלָּתָהּ שֶׁל כְּנֶסֶת-יִשְׂרָאֵל הִיא, שֶׁהִיא מִסְתַּכֶּלֶת עַל הַהֲוָיָה כֻּלָּהּ בָּאַסְפַּקְלַרְיָא הַמְּאִירָה שֶׁל קֹדֶשׁ: בְּכָל עֹז-חַיֶּיהָ הִיא מַכֶּרֶת, שֶׁהַחַיִּים שָׁוִים הֵם אֶת עֶרְכָּם רַק בְּאוֹתָהּ מִדָּה שֶׁהֵם אֱלֹהִיִּים, וְחַיִּים שֶׁאֵינָם אֱלֹהִיִּים אֵינָם שָׁוִים לָהּ מְאוּמָה. הִיא יוֹדַעַת עוֹד, שֶׁבֶּאֱמֶת אֵין חַיִּים אֶלָּא אֱלֹהִיִּים, וְחַיִּים שֶׁאֵינָם אֱלֹהִיִּים אֵינָם חַיִּים כְּלָל, וְהַיְדִיעָה הַזֹּאת, הַמֻּנַחַת בְּעֹמֶק תְּכוּנַת נִשְׁמָתָהּ, מַטְבַּעַת עָלֶיהָ אֶת חוֹתַם-עֶרְכָּהּ הַמְּיֻחָד לָהּ, הַמַּטְבֵּעַ עַל כָּל יָחִיד וְיָחִיד מִיְחִידֶיהָ. כִּי אוֹרוֹ-וְיִשְׁעוֹ שֶׁל הַיָּחִיד תְּלוּיִים הֵם בְּמִדַּת יְדִיעָתוֹ אֶת הִתְעַמְּקוּתוֹ וְהִתְבַּלְּטוּתוֹ שֶׁל הַחוֹתָם הַכְּלָלִי הַזֶּה, שֶׁל הַכָּרַת עֶרֶךְ הַחַיִּים רַק בֶּאֱלֹהִיּוּתָם, בְּתוֹךְ עֹמֶק נִשְׁמָתוֹ. "וְאַתֶּם הַדְּבֵקִים בַּד' אֱלֹהֵיכֶם חַיִּים כֻּלְּכֶם הַיּוֹם " –

---

5. Deut. 4:7. Note that elsewhere, Rav Kook cites this biblical passage explicitly in the context of elaborating the goal of creating an exemplary and enlightened socioeconomic order in Israel. E.g., "In order to fulfill this aspiration, it is particularly necessary that this community possess a political and social state and national sovereignty at the peak of human culture—'surely a wise and understanding people is this great nation'" (Deut. 4:6), *Orot* (Jerusalem: Mossad Harav Kook, 1993), 104.

"For what great nation is there that has a God so close at hand?"[5] What is remarkable about the Jewish people is its ability to view existence through the lens of holiness;[6] it knows, with the full force of its being, that life has the greatest value to the extent that it is infused by godliness and that a life without a touch of the divine is not worth anything. Even more than that, they know that a godly life is true life, and life without God is no life at all. This knowledge, lying deep within the people's soul, gives it a unique character and impresses itself on each and every one of her individual members. The light and salvation of each person depends on the depth and force of this imprinting awareness that the value of life is in its godliness. "And you, who held fast to the Lord your God, are all alive today."[7]

6. Holiness is a central concept in Rav Kook's thought. For an insightful discussion, see Norman Lamm, "Harmonism, Novelty and the Sacred," in *Rabbi Abraham Isaac Kook and Jewish Spirituality*, ed. Lawrence J. Kaplan and David Schatz (New York: New York University Press, 1995), 159–77; see also the introduction to this volume, p.48.

7. Deut. 4:4.

הַחַיִּים, עַ"פ עֵרֶךְ הָאֱלֹהִיּוּת שֶׁבָּהֶם, אֵינָם מִתְגַּלִּים אֶל הַיָּחִיד אֶלָּא
בְּאוֹתָהּ מִדָּה, שֶׁהוּא מִתְאַמֵּץ לִהְיוֹת נִשְׂאָף בְּכָל הֲוָיָתוֹ בְּתוֹכִיּוּתָהּ
שֶׁל כְּלָלוּת הָאֻמָּה, לִהְיוֹת מֻזְהָר מִזֹּהַר נִשְׁמָתָהּ-הָעֶלְיוֹנָה, הַחַיָּה
וְקַיֶּמֶת בְּהַכָּרַת הַיְּקָר הָאֱלֹהִי שֶׁל הַחַיִּים מִתּוֹךְ פְּנִימִיּוּתָהּ הַכְּלָלִית.
טֶבַע הַנְּשָׁמָה הַכְּלָלִית שֶׁל כְּנֶסֶת-יִשְׂרָאֵל הוּא אֱלֹהִיּוּתָהּ. לֹא
בְּחִירָתָהּ גָּרְמָה לָהּ אֶת יִתְרוֹנָהּ הָאֱלֹהִי, לֹא מִצַּד מַעֲשֶׂיהָ הַפְּרָטִיִּים,
לֹא בְּצִדְקָתָהּ וְיֹשֶׁר-לְבָבָהּ בָּאָה אֶל מַעֲלָתָהּ: תְּכוּנַת-גּוּפָהּ, הַגּוּפָנִי
וְהָרוּחָנִי, עָשְׂתָה לָהּ אֶת חֵילָהּ וְאֶת עֻזָּהּ בֵּאלֹהִים, אֲשֶׁר לֹא
בִּבְחִירָה לְקָחָהּ אוֹתוֹ וְלֹא תּוּכַל כָּל קַלְקָלָה שֶׁל בְּחִירָה לְאַבְּדוֹ.
יֵשׁ לָהּ, אָמְנָם, לַהַבְּחִירָה מָבוֹא גָּדוֹל בְּכָל סְגֻלָּה טִבְעִית, בִּהְיוֹתָהּ
טוֹבָה תּוּכַל לְפַנְּקָהּ, לְעַדְּנָהּ, לְהוֹצִיאָהּ לַפֹּעַל בְּאֹפֶן שָׁלֵם וְחָשׁוּב,
וְכֵן בִּהְיוֹתָהּ רָעָה וּשְׁפָלָה תּוּכַל לְהַחֲשִׁיךְ אֶת הַמָּאוֹר שֶׁבַּסְּגֻלָּה
הַטִּבְעִית וְלַעֲכֹּר אֶת זֹהֲרוֹ, לְטַמְטֵם אֶת הַלֵּב לְבַל יָחוּשׁ אֶת הָעֹשֶׁר

---

8. Rav Kook uses the word *neshama* here for "soul." This is the highest of the
    three levels of soul that are commonly discussed by the kabbalists: *nefesh*,
    ruah, and *neshama*. See the introduction to this volume, p. 53.

9. The nature of the Jewish people's difference from other nations is a classic
    issue in Jewish thought; the key medieval protagonists were Yehuda Halevi
    and Maimonides. See introduction to this volume for further discussion of
    Rav Kook's relation to their views, p.52.

10. Rav Kook expresses here in brief his view that the holiness of Israel depends
    on two main elements: an innate *segula*, or soul force; and the choices to do
    good or bad that each of us makes. He believed that the *segula* force was the

Life in its fullest, divine intensity is increasingly revealed to a person to the extent that he struggles to aspire with all his being to connect to the inner life of the people as a whole and to be illuminated by the light of its exalted spirit; the spirit lives through a pervasive inner awareness of the precious godliness in life.

The essential quality of the Jewish people's collective soul is its divine nature.[8] The people did not gain this characteristic[9] through its choices, actions, righteousness, or good character. It is a core quality, both physical and spiritual, that gives the people divine force and strength. It was not acquired through choice, and no choices can negate it. Choices, however, can powerfully affect the state of this innate quality.[10] The people can decide to nurture, develop, and perfect it; alternatively, bad choices will darken its light, muddy its glow, and stupefy hearts so that they will no longer sense the spiritual riches hidden in the life of the soul. But darkness and stupefaction

greater and that it would grow stronger still in the period of the "footsteps of the Messiah." See *Igerot hare'aya* 2:186–88 (Jerusalem: Mossad Harav Kook, 2002), for an expanded discussion of this. For a good English summary, see Michael Z. Nehorai, "Halakhah, Meta-Halakhah, and the Redemption of Israel: Reflections on the Rabbinic Rulings of Rav Kook," in *Rabbi Abraham Isaac Kook and Jewish Spirituality*, ed. Kaplan and Schatz, 122–24.

הָרוּחָנִי הַצָּפוּן בְּתוֹךְ חַיֵּי-הַנְּשָׁמָה. אֲבָל לֹא יוּכְלוּ טִמְטוּם-הַלֵּב
וְהַחְשָׁכַת הַמָּאוֹר לְהִמָּשֵׁךְ לְעוֹלָם. הַסְּגֻלָּה הַטִּבְעִית בְּטוּחָה הִיא
בְּקִיּוּמָהּ וּבְהִתְעוֹרְרוּתָהּ לִתְחִיָּה.

סְגֻלַּת הָאֻמָּה, - הַטּוֹב הָאֱלֹהִי הַטָּבוּעַ בְּקִרְבָּהּ, סֵדֶר-הָעוֹלָם, הַחַיִּים
הַיְשָׁרִים וְהַטּוֹבִים הַמַּתְאִימִים אֶל הַצֶּדֶק וְהַיֹּשֶׁר, הַשֶּׁקֶט וְהַשַּׁלְוָה,
הַחֵן וְהָאֹמֶץ הַמְמֻלָּאִים בְּהִסְתַּכְּלוּת אֱלֹהִית מַקֶּפֶת, כְּפִי מַה שֶׁהִיא
נִמְצֵאת בְּנִשְׁמַת-הָאֻמָּה, - אֵין חַיֵּי הַחֹל יְכוֹלִים לְהוֹצִיאָהּ מִן הַכֹּחַ
אֶל הַפֹּעַל. חַיִּים אֵלֶּה בִּמְהוּמָתָם הַמַּעֲשִׂית הַתְּכוּפָה מַסְתִּירִים
הֵם אֶת הַהוֹד הָרוּחָנִי שֶׁל הַנְּשָׁמָה הָאֱלֹהִית, וּמְעַכְּבִים אֶת הַזְרָחַת
אוֹרָהּ הַבָּהִיר וְהַיָּשָׁר לְתוֹךְ הַמְּצִיאוּת הַחֻלּוֹנִית הַשּׁוֹלֶטֶת. דְּחִיפַת
הַגִּדּוּל וְהַהִשְׁתַּלְמוּת שֶׁל הַחַיִּים צְרִיכָה שֶׁתֵּצֵא אֶל הַפֹּעַל עַל-יְדֵי
נְתִינַת-רֶוַח, שֶׁל הַפְסָקָה וְהִתְנַעֲרוּת, מִמְּהוּמַת-הַחַיִּים הָרְגִילָה.
הַיָּחִיד מִתְנַעֵר מֵחַיֵּי-הַחֹל לִפְרָקִים קְרוֹבִים, - בְּכָל שַׁבָּת. "בָּא
שַׁבָּת בָּאָה מְנוּחָה", מַתְחֶלֶת הַנֶּפֶשׁ לְהִשְׁתַּחְרֵר מִכְּבָלֶיהָ הַקָּשִׁים,
"בְּיוֹם הָנִיחַ ד' לָךְ מֵעָצְבְּךָ וּמֵרָגְזֶךָ וּמִן הָעֲבֹדָה הַקָּשָׁה אֲשֶׁר עֻבַּד
בָּךְ", וּמְבַקֶּשֶׁת הִיא לָהּ אָז נְתִיבוֹת עֶלְיוֹנוֹת, חֲפָצִים רוּחָנִיִּים, כְּפִי

11. The inevitability of spiritual renewal is a theme of Rav Kook's book on repentance, *Orot hateshuva* (Jerusalem: Rabbi Kook Institute, 1994). See e.g.,
chap. 1, where repentance is described as a natural health-restoring impulse;
4:2, where the repentance of the individual is an expression of a movement
toward *teshuva* active in the whole universe; and 16:10, where the individual's
teshuva is presented as a return to authentic selfhood.

cannot continue indefinitely. Sooner or later, this inner soul treasure can be relied upon to arouse the nation to renewal.[11]

This national treasure that is imprinted deep within us, the image of a world that is good, upright, and godly—aligned with peace, justice, grace, and courage, all filled with a pervasive divine perspective that rests in the spirit of the people—cannot be actualized within a way of life that is purely secular. Such a life, full of frenetic action, veils the glory of our divine soul, and the soul's clear light is blocked from shining through the overpowering, mundane reality. The impulse toward growth and self-realization needs space to come to fruition. We need to stop and shake off the bedlam of our daily lives.

The individual shakes off mundane routine frequently—every week. "Shabbat comes and so does rest!"[12] The soul begins to shed her harsh chains. "The Lord has given you rest from your sorrow and trouble and from the hard service that you were made to serve."[13] The soul then seeks higher pathways of spiritual desire that are

12.   Rashi on Gen. 2:2. Rashi's full comment reads: "What was lacking [in Creation]? Rest. Enter Sabbath, enter rest; and then the work of Creation was finished." Creation was not complete until rest was made to complement and balance creative activity.

13.   Isa. 14:3.

טֶבַע-מְקוֹרָה, "טוֹב לְהֹדוֹת לַד' וּלְזַמֵּר לְשִׁמְךָ עֶלְיוֹן. לְהַגִּיד בַּבֹּקֶר חַסְדֶּךָ וֶאֱמוּנָתְךָ בַּלֵּילוֹת. עֲלֵי עָשׂוֹר וַעֲלֵי נָבֶל עֲלֵי הִגָּיוֹן בְּכִנּוֹר." "בֵּינִי וּבֵין בְּנֵי יִשְׂרָאֵל אוֹת הִוא לְעֹלָם!" יוֹם קָדוֹשׁ, אֲשֶׁר בּוֹ תִּתְגַּלֶּה נְטִיַּת הָאֻמָּה – הַנְּטִיָּה שֶׁל הַחַיִּים הָאֱלֹהִיִּים כְּמוֹ שֶׁהֵם – בִּיחִידֶיהָ, אוֹת הִיא לָאֻמָּה שֶׁיֵּשׁ בִּסְגֻלַּת נִשְׁמָתָהּ צֹרֶךְ וִיכֹלֶת לְהִתְעַנֵּג עַל ד', - וְנֹעַם אֱלֹהִי, הַמִּתְכַּנֵּס לִנְקֻדָּה רוּחָנִית שֶׁל נְשָׁמָה-יְתֵרָה, שָׁרוּי בְּלִבּוֹ שֶׁל כָּל יָחִיד מִבָּנֶיהָ.

אֶת אוֹתָהּ הַפְּעוּלָה, שֶׁהַשַּׁבָּת פּוֹעֶלֶת עַל כָּל יָחִיד, פּוֹעֶלֶת הִיא הַשְּׁמִטָּה עַל הָאֻמָּה בִּכְלָלָהּ. צֹרֶךְ מְיֻחָד הוּא לָאֻמָּה זוֹ, שֶׁהַיְצִירָה הָאֱלֹהִית נְטוּעָה בְּקִרְבָּהּ בְּאֹפֶן בּוֹלֵט וְנִצְחִי, כִּי מִזְּמַן לִזְמַן יִתְגַּלֶּה בְּתוֹכָהּ הַמָּאוֹר הָאֱלֹהִי שֶׁלָּהּ בְּכָל מְלֹא זָהֳרוֹ, אֲשֶׁר לֹא יַשְׁבִּיתוּהוּ חַיֵּי-הַחֶבְרָה-שֶׁל-חוֹל עִם הֶעָמָל וְהַדְּאָגָה, הַזַּעַף וְהַתַּחֲרוּת אֲשֶׁר

---

14. Ps. 92:1–4. This is the "Psalm for the Sabbath Day."

15. Exod. 31:17.

16. Rav Kook refers to the "extra soul" that, according to tradition, Jews possess on the Sabbath. The talmudic source is Beitza 16a, which interprets the words *shavat vayinafash* (Exod. 31:17) as *Vay nefesh!* ("Alas for the soul that is lost!"— at the end of Sabbath). Interpretations of this idea have ranged from the more rational, e.g., Ibn Ezra and Radak, who argue that the soul that "is given rest on this day from the affairs of the world can occupy itself with wisdom and the words of God" (commentary to Gen. 2:3), to the more mystical, e.g., Naḥmanides, who takes issue with Ibn Ezra and writes that "although his view of this is

consonant with the nature of her source. "It is good to praise the Lord, to sing hymns to Your name, O Most High, to proclaim Your steadfast love at daybreak, Your faithfulness each night with a ten-stringed harp with voice and lyre together."[14] "It shall be a sign for all time between me and the people of Israel."[15] This is a holy day when the innate inclination of the people for a godly life emerges from its hiddenness and is a sign for the people that its soul treasure contains within it the need and the ability to rejoice in God, in the delight of the divine. This is concentrated in the point of the extra soul[16] that dwells within each one of the people's children.

What Sabbath does for the individual, shmita does for the nation as a whole. The Jewish people, in whom the godly, creative force is planted eternally and distinctively, has a special need to periodically reveal the divine light within itself with full intensity. Our mundane lives, with their toil, anxiety, anger, and competition do not entirely suffocate this creative force. On the shmita, our pure,

right to those who believe in it, for this is not something that can be tested by experience, … nonetheless you must understand that on the Sabbath, there is in truth an additional soul." (See also Zohar II 204a–b.) Rav Kook draws on elements of both schools here in understanding the "extra soul" as something that is always within us that we are able to access on Sabbath when the rush of weekday activity is stilled.

לָהֶם, לְמַעַן תּוּכַל לְהִתְגַּלּוֹת בְּקִרְבָּהּ פְּנִימָה טָהֳרַת נִשְׁמָתָהּ
בִּכְלָלוּתָהּ כְּמוֹ-שֶׁהִיא. וְאִם אוֹתָהּ הָאַבִּירִיּוּת, הַמֻּכְרַחַת לְהִתְלַוּוֹת
עִם כָּל סֵדֶר שֶׁל חַיֵּי-צִבּוּר קְבוּעִים, גּוֹרֶמֶת לְהַקְטִין אֶת עֲדִינוּת-
הַחַיִּים הַמּוּסָרִית, וְהַנִּגּוּד, הַמַּתְמִיד שֶׁבֵּין הַשְּׁמִיעָה הָאִידֵיאָלִית
לְהַכְרָזָה שֶׁל חֶסֶד וֶאֱמֶת, חֶמְלָה וְרַחֲמִים, לְבֵין הַנִּגִּישָׁה וְהַכְּפִיָּה
וְלַחַץ הַקְּפָדָה שֶׁל קִנְיָן וּרְכוּשׁ, הַמֻּכְרָחִים לְהֵרָאוֹת בָּעוֹלָם הַמַּעֲשִׂי,
גּוֹרֵם הַרְחָקָה לָאוֹר הָאֱלֹהִי מִתְּכוּנַת הַכָּרָתָהּ הַצִּבּוּרִית שֶׁל הָאֻמָּה,
שֶׁהַרְחָקָה זוֹ מִפַּעְפַּעַת כְּאָרֶס גַּם בְּמוּסָרָם שֶׁל הַיְחִידִים, - הִנֵּה
הַפְסָקַת הַסֵּדֶר הַחֶבְרָתִי בִּצְדָדִים יְדוּעִים, מִתְּקוּפָה לִתְקוּפָה,
מְבִיאָה לָאֻמָּה זוֹ, כְּשֶׁהִיא מְסֻדֶּרֶת, עַל מְכוֹנָהּ, לִידֵי עֲלִיָּתָהּ הָעַצְמִית
לִמְרוֹמֵי הַתְּכוּנוֹת הַפְּנִימִיּוֹת שֶׁבַּחַיִּים הַמּוּסָרִיִּים וְהָרוּחָנִיִּים, מִצַּד
הַתֹּכֶן הָאֱלֹהִי שֶׁבָּהֶם, הָעוֹמֵד לְמַעְלָה לְמַעְלָה מִכָּל תַּכְסִיס וְסֵדֶר
חֶבְרָתִי וְהוּא מְעַבֵּד וּמַעֲלֶה אֶת הַסְּדָרִים הַחֶבְרָתִיִּים וְנוֹתֵן לָהֶם
אֶת שְׁלֵמוּתָם. –

17. There is a note of suspicion about commerce in this passage. For a discussion
of Rav Kook's relationship to socialist thought, see Shalom Rosenberg, "Introduction to the Thought of Rav Kook," in *The World of Rav Kook's Thought*,
ed. Benjamin Ish-Shalom and Shalom Rosenberg (Jerusalem: Avi Chai,
1991), 59–61. See also the introduction to this volume, p.49.

inner spirit may be revealed as it truly is. The forcefulness
that is inevitably part of our regular, public lives lessens
our moral refinement. There is always a tension between
the ideal of listening to the voice inside us that calls
us to be kind, truthful, and merciful, and the conflict,
compulsion, and pressure to be unyielding that surround
buying, selling, and acquiring things.[17] These aspects
of the world of action distance us from the divine light
and prevent its being discerned in the public life of the
nation. This distancing also permeates the morality of
individuals like poison. Stilling the tumult of social life
from time to time in certain predictable ways is meant to
move this nation, when it is well-ordered, to rise toward
an encounter with the heights of its other, inner moral
and spiritual life.[18] They touch the divine qualities inside
them that transcend all the stratagems of the social order
and that cultivate and elevate our social arrangements,
bringing them toward perfection.

18. Cf. Rav Kook's idea of "the continuous prayer of the soul": the soul is always
praying (i.e., yearning to unite with God). When we consciously pray, we rise
to an encounter with the soul that is praying constantly (*Olat hare'aya*, 1:1).

"וּכְשֵׁם שֶׁנֶּאֱמַר בְּשַׁבַּת בְּרֵאשִׁית 'שַׁבָּת לַד' כָּךְ נֶאֱמַר בַּשְּׁבִיעִית:
שַׁבָּת לַד'." סְגֻלַּת הָאָרֶץ וּסְגֻלַּת הָאֻמָּה מַתְאִימוֹת יַחַד. כְּשֵׁם
שֶׁהָאֻמָּה הִיא מְיֻחֶדֶת לָרוֹמְמוּת הָאֱלֹהִית בְּמַעֲמַקֵּי חַיֶּיהָ, כָּךְ
הָאָרֶץ, אֶרֶץ ד', הִיא מַכְשִׁירָה אֶת הָעָם הַיּוֹשֵׁב עָלֶיהָ בְּנַחֲלַת
עוֹלָמִים, הַבָּאָה בִּבְרִית וּבִשְׁבוּעָה בְּבִטָּחוֹן נֵצַח יִשְׂרָאֵל, הַמְיֻסָּד
עַל הַטֶּבַע הָאֱלֹהִי הַקָּבוּעַ בְּמַטְבֵּעַ אֶרֶץ-חֶמְדָּה נִפְלָאָה זוֹ, הַמְזֻוֶּגֶת
לָעָם זֶה אֲשֶׁר בָּחַר לוֹ יָהּ לִסְגֻלָּתוֹ. נִשְׁמַת הָאֻמָּה וְהָאָרֶץ יַחְדָּו
פּוֹעֲלוֹת אֶת יְסוֹד הֲוָיָתָן, תּוֹבְעוֹת אֶת תַּפְקִידָן, לְהוֹצִיא אֶל הַפֹּעַל
אֶת עֲרִיגַת קְדֻשָּׁתָן, בִּשְׁנַת-שַׁבָּתוֹן. הָעָם פּוֹעֵל בְּכֹחוֹ הַנַּפְשִׁי עַל
הָאָרֶץ, זְרוֹעַ ד' מִתְגַּלָּה עַל-יְדֵי הַשְׁפָּעָתוֹ הָרוּחָנִית, וְהָאָרֶץ פּוֹעֶלֶת
עַל הָעָם, לְהַכְשִׁיר אֶת תְּכוּנָתוֹ לְפִי חֵפֶץ חַיִּים אֱלֹהִיִּים שְׁלֵמִים
בְּתַבְנִיתָם.

‐ שְׁנַת שַׁבָּתוֹן מְכַרַחַת הִיא לָאֻמָּה וְלָאָרֶץ!

שְׁנַת שֶׁקֶט וְשַׁלְוָה, בְּאֵין נוֹגֵשׂ וְרוֹדֶה, "לֹא יִגֹּשׂ אֶת רֵעֵהוּ וְאֶת
אָחִיו כִּי קָרָא שְׁמִטָּה לַד'," שְׁנַת שִׁוְיוֹן וּמַרְגּוֹעַ, הִתְפַּשְּׁטוּת הַנִּשְׁמָה
בְּהַרְחָבָתָהּ אֶל הַיֹּשֶׁר הָאֱלֹהִי הַמְכַלְכֵּל חַיִּים בְּחֶסֶד, אֵין רְכוּשׁ פְּרָטִי
מְסֻיָּם וְלֹא זְכוּת קַפְּדָנִית, וְשָׁלוֹם אֱלֹהִי שׁוֹרֵר עַל כָּל אֲשֶׁר נְשָׁמָה
בְּאַפּוֹ. "וְהָיְתָה שַׁבַּת הָאָרֶץ לָכֶם לְאָכְלָה לְךָ וּלְעַבְדְּךָ וְלַאֲמָתֶךָ

---

19. Rashi's commentary on Lev. 25:2.

20. Deut. 15:2. The verse quoted refers to the remission of debts in the shmita and prohibits creditors from exacting payment from debtors.

"Just as it was said about the Sabbath of creation, 'it is a Sabbath for God,' so, too, it was said about the Sabbath of shmita, 'it is a Sabbath for God.'"[19] The distinctive character of the people and the land dovetail with each other. Just as the people has a special aptitude for reaching spiritual heights from within the depths of everyday life, so, too, the land—God's land—forms the people who dwell there as an everlasting inheritance that comes through a covenant and promise, with faith in the Eternal One of Israel, and is founded on the divine nature immovably infused in this wonderful country, which is married to the people whom God chose. The soul of the people and the land intertwine, working from the basis of their being to bring into existence the intricate patterns of inner holiness that lie within them during the sabbatical year. The people works with its soul force on the land, and the divine seed is revealed through its spiritual influence; the land, too, works on the people, refining their character in line with the divine desire for life inherent in their makeup.

The people and the land both need a year of Sabbath!

A year of peace and quiet, where there are no tyrants or taskmasters; "he shall not oppress his fellow or kinsman, for the remission proclaimed is of the Lord";[20] a year of equality and relaxation in which the soul may expand

וְלִשְׂכִירְךָ וּלְתוֹשָׁבְךָ הַגָּרִים עִמָּךְ, וְלִבְהֶמְתְּךָ וְלַחַיָּה אֲשֶׁר בְּאַרְצֶךָ תִּהְיֶה כָל תְּבוּאָתָהּ לֶאֱכֹל." אֵין חִלּוּל-קֹדֶשׁ שֶׁל קַפְּדָנוּת רְכוּשׁ פְּרָטִי בְּכָל תּוֹצָאוֹת-יְבוּלָהּ שֶׁל שָׁנָה זוֹ, וְחֶמְדַּת-הָעֹשֶׁר, הַמִּתְגָּרָה עַל-יְדֵי הַמִּסְחָר, מִשְׁתַּתַּחַת "לְאָכְלָה - וְלֹא לִסְחוֹרָה". עַיִן-טוֹבָה וְהוֹקָרָה נֶאֱמָנָה בָּאָה לְכָל בִּרְכַּת ד' אֲשֶׁר בִּפְרִי-הָאָרֶץ, "לְאָכְלָה - וְלֹא לְהֶפְסֵד". וְהָאָדָם חוֹזֵר אֶל טִבְעוֹ הָרַעֲנָן, עַד אֲשֶׁר לֹא יִצְטָרֵךְ לִרְפוּאוֹת לְמַחֲלוֹת, שֶׁהֵן בָּאוֹת בְּרֻבָּן עַל-יְדֵי הֲרִיסַת הַמִּשְׁקָל שֶׁל הַחַיִּים, בְּהִתְרַחֲקָם מִטָּהֳרַת הַטֶּבַע הָרוּחָנִי וְהַחָמְרִי "לְאָכְלָה - וְלֹא לִמְלוּגְמָא, וְלֹא לִרְפוּאָה, וְלֹא לַעֲשׂוֹת מִמֶּנָּה אֲפִיקְטְוֹזִין". רוּחַ קֹדֶשׁ וַאֲצִילוּת שָׁפוּךְ עַל פְּנֵי כָל, "שְׁנַת שַׁבָּתוֹן יִהְיֶה לָאָרֶץ, - שַׁבָּת לַד'"!.

21. Lev. 25:5–7.

22. Mishnah, Shevi'it 7:3. In this passage, Rav Kook draws on a series of halakhic midrashim based on a phrase from Lev. 25:6, "for you to eat," which is interpreted to exclude making use of food grown in the Land of Israel during the shmita for purposes other than eating.

23. Talmud Bavli, Sukkah 40a. See the introduction to this volume for further discussion of Rav Kook's astonishing claim that shmita will promote a natural state of human health that will make medicine unnecessary.

24. Lev. 25:4–5.

toward the uprightness of God, who sustains all life with loving-kindness; a year when there is no private property and no standing on one's rights, and a godly peace will pervade all that breathes. "It shall be a year of complete rest for the land, but you may eat whatever the land will produce during its Sabbath—you, your male and female slaves, the hired and bound laborers who live with you, and your cattle and the beasts on your land may eat all its yield."[21] Pernickety claims to private property will not profane the holiness of the produce of the land during this year, and the urge to get rich, which is stimulated by trade, will be forgotten; as it says, "for you to eat—but not for your trade."[22] A spirit of generosity will rest on all; God will bless the fruit of the land "for you to eat and not your loss." Human beings will return to a state of natural health, so that they will not need healing for sicknesses, which mostly befall us when the balance of life is destroyed and our lives are distanced from the rhythms of nature; "for you to eat" but not to make medicine and not to use as bandages.[23] A holy spirit will be poured out upon all life; "it will be a year of complete rest for the land—a Sabbath of the Lord."[24]

בְּשָׁנָה זוֹ מִתְגַּלָּה צִבְיוֹנָהּ שֶׁל הָאֻמָּה בִּכְלִיל הוֹדָהּ, בִּמְקוֹר רוּחָהּ הָאֱלֹהִי. וְהָאָרָה זוֹ, הַבָּאָה לְשֶׁבַע שָׁנִים, מוֹשֶׁכֶת אַחֲרֶיהָ עִלִּיּוֹת אִידֵאָלִיּוֹת אֱלֹהִיּוֹת, שֶׁבְּהִכָּשְׁרָן הָאִטִּי שֶׁל הַנְּשָׁמוֹת הֵן הוֹלְכוֹת וְכוֹבְשׁוֹת לָהֶן מָקוֹם בַּחַיִּים, עַד שֶׁהַהַשְׁקָפוֹת-הַחַיִּים הַנּוֹבְעוֹת מִמֶּנָּה נַעֲשׂוֹת יוֹתֵר וְיוֹתֵר קְבוּעוֹת וּמְסֻיָּמוֹת וּפוֹעֲלוֹת, עַד בֹּא תְּקוּפָה יוֹתֵר אֲרֻכָּה, יוֹתֵר חֲשׁוּבָה, שֶׁהִיא מַסְפֶּקֶת כְּבָר לְהַעֲלוֹת לֹא אֶת אִישֵׁי-הָאֻמָּה הַיְחִידִים וְלֹא רַק אֶת כְּלָלוּתָהּ בַּדּוֹר הַהֹוֶה הַיְחִידִי כִּי-אִם אֶת הַדּוֹרוֹת שֶׁלָּהּ. – הַיּוֹבֵל, זוֹהִי תְּקוּפָה הֲרַת-עוֹלָם, הָעֲרוּכָה מִיְּסוֹד הַחֵפֶץ הָאֱלֹהִי הָעֶלְיוֹן.

סֵדֶר-הַחַיִּים שֶׁל שְׁנַת הַשְּׁמִטָּה הוּא עַל-פִּי הַחֵפֶץ הַפְּנִימִי הַטִּבְעִי שֶׁל תְּשׁוּקַת הַטּוֹב וְהַצֶּדֶק, הַשִּׁוְיוֹן וְהַמְּנוּחָה, שֶׁהַהַכָּרָה הָאֱלֹהִית וּתְשׁוּקָתָהּ מַטְבִּיעָה בְּקֶרֶב הָאֻמָּה, אֲשֶׁר אֵין זֶה לָהּ תְּכוּנָה חֲקוּיִית, דָּבָר מְלֻמָּד מִן הַחוּץ, כִּי-אִם נַחֲלָתָהּ הַטִּבְעִית מִמְּקוֹרָהּ עַצְמָהּ. אֲבָל מְקוֹר יִשְׂרָאֵל כְּשֶׁמִּתְגַּלֶּה בְּטָהֳרוֹ אֵינֶנּוּ עוֹמֵד עַל עָמְדוֹ, מִתְגַּבֵּר הוּא תָּמִיד וּמִתְרַחֵב וְהוֹלֵךְ. מַקְנֶה הוּא לְעַצְמוֹ אֶת אֹמֶץ הַפְּעֻלָּה וְכֹחַ הַהַשְׁפָּעָה וְסוֹפֵג לְתוֹכוֹ אֶת הָעִלּוּי שֶׁל הַבְּחִירָה הַטּוֹבָה, הַתְּשׁוּבָה הַטְּהוֹרָה, הַמִּתְגַּבֶּרֶת בְּתִגְבֹּרֶת הָאֱלֹהִיּוּת שֶׁל הַחַיִּים כְּפִי מְקוֹר יִשְׂרָאֵל . נִמְשָׁךְ הוּא וְהוֹלֵךְ בִּקְדֻשָּׁתוֹ בְּכָל מֶשֶׁךְ הַזְּמַן שֶׁל הַפְּרָקִים, "מוֹנִין שְׁמִיטִין לְקַדֵּשׁ יוֹבְלִין," לְהַכְשִׁיר אֵלָיו

In this year, the divine character within the people will
be revealed in its glory. This once-every-seven-year
illumination carries an afterglow of divine ideals that will
gradually shape our ethical characters so that the outlook
that flows from them will become a deeper and more
formative part of us, until a longer, significant period has
elapsed—enough to raise up not merely individuals[25]—or
just the collective in a particular generation[26] but all the
generations that lived during that period. The Jubilee is a
time of rebirth for the whole world, grounded in divine
freedom.

Life during the shmita year is guided by the natural, inner
desire for goodness and justice, equality, and calm, which
God has planted within the nation. The people did not
become like this by imitating something external; it is part
of its nature. When this inner life starts to reveal itself
in all its purity, it does not stand still. It is expansive and
generous, seeking the power to act and to influence its
surroundings. Israel's inner nature soaks up the elevating
power of its good choices, which restore our lives and the
pure penitence that reconnects us to the source of the
Jewish people's inner strength. Holiness grows throughout
these spans of time: "Count the shmita years in order to

25.   As does the Sabbath.

26.   As does the shmita.

אֶת הַחַיִּים. "וְסָפַרְתָּ לְךָ שֶׁבַע שַׁבְּתֹת שָׁנִים שֶׁבַע שָׁנִים שֶׁבַע
פְּעָמִים וְהָיוּ לְךָ יְמֵי שֶׁבַע שַׁבְּתֹת הַשָּׁנִים תֵּשַׁע וְאַרְבָּעִים שָׁנָה."
וּמְצֻנּוֹר-הַחַיִּים שֶׁל הַיּוֹבֵל, שֶׁהוּא הוֹלֵךְ בְּמַעֲלוֹת שְׁלַבָּיו וּמִתְפַּשֵּׁט
עַד בּאוֹ אֶל חַיֵּי הָאֻמָּה בְּצִבְיוֹנָם הַפְּרָטִי, יוֹנֶקֶת הִיא הַשְּׁמִטָּה
וּמִתְמַלֵּאת אֶת זִיוָהּ הַשָּׁלֵם וְהָרַעֲנָן, - הַמִּתְגַּלֶּה בָּהּ מִתְּשׁוּקָתָהּ
אֶל הַסֵּדֶר הָאֱלֹהִי שֶׁיָּחוּל בִּמְלֹא כָל הַיְקוּם וְלֹא רַק בְּקִרְבָּהּ פְּנִימָה,
לְבַדָּהּ. וְהוֹלֵךְ וּמִתְעַלֶּה הוּא הָרוּחַ, עַד שֶׁנִּצְבַּר כֹּחַ גָּדוֹל וְעָצוּם,
שֶׁיֵּשׁ בּוֹ דֵּי אוֹנִים לֹא רַק לְגַלּוֹת אֶת הַטּוֹב שֶׁיֶּשְׁנוֹ בִּמְזֻמָּן בְּאוֹצַר
חַיֵּי הָאֻמָּה, לִשְׁמוֹר אֶת צִבְיוֹן-הַחַיִּים, כְּמִדָּתָהּ שֶׁל הַשְּׁמִטָּה, כִּי-
אִם גַּם לְיַשֵּׁר אֶת הַמַּעֲקַשִּׁים וְהַקִּלְקוּלִים שֶׁל הֶעָבָר וּלְהַעֲמִיד אֶת
מַצָּב חַיֵּי הָאֻמָּה עַ"פ הֲוָיָתָהּ הַמְּקוֹרִית, לַהֲשִׁיבָם לִימֵי-הָעֲלוּמִים
בְּרַעֲנַנּוּת מַטְעָה, וּלְגַלּוֹת לֹא רַק מַה שֶׁגָּנוּז בְּטִבְעָהּ שֶׁל נִשְׁמַת
הָאֻמָּה בְּפֹעַל כִּי-אִם מַה שֶּׁמֻּכְשָׁר לְהִגָּלוֹת וּלְהָאִיר בְּקִרְבָּהּ, עַל-
יְדֵי עֶזְרַת הִתְגַּלּוּת הַהַטָּבָה הַבְּחִירִית שֶׁלָּהּ, שֶׁהִיא צְרִיכָה לְהָעִיר
אֶת הַהִתְרוֹמְמוּת הַיּוֹבְלִית.

הָאֻמָּה נוֹתֶנֶת אוֹת, שֶׁהַכְשִׁירָה אֶת עַצְמָהּ, בִּימֵי הִתְגַּלּוּת סְגֻלָּתָהּ
הַטִּבְעִית, אֶל הָעֶלְיוֹנִיּוּת הָרוֹמֲמָה הַזֹּאת, שֶׁכְּשֶׁרוֹנָהּ יוּכַל לְהַגִּיעַ

---

27. Talmud Bavli, Arakhin 32b. The Talmud describes here how the advent of the
     Jubilee was to be calculated.

28. Lev. 25:8.

sanctify the Jubilees,"[27] to prepare life for the Jubilee. "And
you shall count off seven weeks of seven years—seven
times seven years—so that the period of seven weeks of
seven years gives you a total of forty-nine years."[28] Shmita
will suckle from the life channels of the Jubilee, which
will gradually rise and spread, until they give shape to the
life of the people. From those sources will the shmita be
filled with a wholesome and invigorating glow that will
arise out of the yearning for a divine order that fills all
existence and not merely its own inner being.

The spirit of the Jubilee will gather great strength, until
it has sufficient potency not only to reveal the goodness
within the soul of the people and protect its form of life,
as does the shmita, but also to fix the crookedness and
brokenness of the past and to reestablish the people's
existence on its original pattern. It can restore a pristine
freshness to our lives, not only through what is already
present, albeit hidden in our souls, but also through what
is being prepared to reveal itself and illuminate us by the
power of our free choice to do what is good—which must
awaken in the exalted Jubilee year.

In these years, when its inner character is being revealed,
the nation gives a sign that it is preparing itself for an
even higher level; one that can lead to a keen awareness

לָהּ בַּהַכָּרָה הַנִּשְׂגָּבָה שֶׁל אֱלֹהִיּוּת הַחַיִּים, וְהַהַכָּרָה מִתְעוֹרֶרֶת,
שֶׁיֵּשׁ רוּחַ חֲדָשָׁה הַמְּבַשֶּׂרֶת צְבָא רַב, "וְהַעֲבַרְתָּ שׁוֹפַר תְּרוּעָה
בַּחֹדֶשׁ הַשְּׁבִיעִי בֶּעָשׂוֹר לַחֹדֶשׁ בְּיוֹם הַכִּפֻּרִים תַּעֲבִירוּ שׁוֹפָר בְּכָל
אַרְצְכֶם." רוּחַ אֵל עֶלְיוֹן שֶׁל הַסְּלִיחָה הַכְּלָלִית, הַפּוֹשֶׁטֶת אֶת כָּל
יָחִיד בְּכָל יוֹם הַכִּפֻּרִים, מִתְעַלָּה כָּאן בִּקְדֻשַּׁת הַיּוֹבֵל לִצְבְיוֹן כְּלָלִי,
בְּהִתְלַבֵּשׁ הָאֻמָּה בְּרוּחַ סְלִיחָה וּתְשׁוּבָה לְיַשֵּׁר אֶת כָּל עֲווֹתֵי הֶעָבַר.
"וּקְרָאתֶם דְּרוֹר בָּאָרֶץ לְכָל יֹשְׁבֶיהָ," "מָר"ה עַד יוֹם-הַכִּפּוּרִים
לֹא הָיוּ עֲבָדִים נִפְטָרִים לְבָתֵּיהֶם וְלֹא מִשְׁתַּעְבְּדִים לַאֲדוֹנֵיהֶם.
אֶלָּא אוֹכְלִין וְשׁוֹתִין וּשְׂמֵחִין וְעַטְרוֹתֵיהֶן בְּרָאשֵׁיהֶן. כֵּיוָן שֶׁהִגִּיעַ
יוֹם הַכִּפּוּרִים תָּקְעוּ ב"ד בַּשּׁוֹפָר, נִפְטְרוּ עֲבָדִים לְבָתֵּיהֶן וְשָׂדוֹת
חוֹזְרוֹת לְבַעֲלֵיהֶן" (רֹאשׁ הַשָּׁנָה ח:). אֵין הַדְּרוֹר הַזֶּה פּוֹרֵץ כְּהַר-
פְּרָצִים, כִּי נִמְשָׁךְ וְהוֹלֵךְ הוּא מִן הַקֹּדֶשׁ הָעֶלְיוֹן, אֵינֶנּוּ יוֹצֵא בְּתוֹר
יוֹצֵא-דֹפֶן מִתּוֹךְ הַמַּעְגָּל הַחֶבְרָתִי הַמְסֻדָּר, כִּי מִתּוֹכוֹ וּמֵעַצְמוּתוֹ
הוּא נוֹבֵעַ, מִתּוֹךְ סֵדֶר-הַחַיִּים שֶׁל הַתְּקוּפוֹת הַקְּצָרוֹת הַקְּדוּמוֹת,
עַד הַגִּיעוֹ לִידֵי מִדָּתוֹ זוֹ, שֶׁהוּא מַתְחִיל לְהִתְרוֹמֵם בְּפָעֳלַת כִּשְׁרוֹנָהּ
שֶׁל הָאֻמָּה בְּהִתְגַּלּוּתָהּ הַבְּחִירִית, - בְּתִקּוּן הָעֲווֹתִים שֶׁל הֶעָבַר.

---

29. Lev. 25:9.

30. Lev. 25:10.

31. Talmud Bavli, Rosh Hashanah 8b. See the introduction to this volume for a discussion of Rav Kook's original reading of this talmudic passage.

of the godliness in life. The awakening of such awareness heralds a new spirit that announces great things: "Then you shall sound the horn loud; in the seventh month on the tenth day of the month—the Day of Atonement—you shall have the horn sounded throughout your land,"[29] and a godly spirit of general forgiveness, such as the individual experiences on Yom Kippur, will arise through the holiness of the Jubilee and spread throughout the entire society, clothing the whole people in a spirit of repentance and acquittal that will straighten out the injustices of the preceding period: "You shall proclaim release throughout the land for all its inhabitants."[30] From Rosh Hashanah until Yom Kippur, slaves would neither become free to go home, nor would they remain slaves to their masters, but they would eat, drink, and rejoice with crowns on their heads. When Yom Kippur would arrive, the *beit din* would sound the shofar, slaves would be free to go home, and fields would return to their original owners.[31] This freedom does not erupt like some volcano; it emerges gradually from the higher holiness. It is not a radical exception to the regular social order but flows from within it, nurtured by the life of the shorter, preceding periods until, reinforced by the revelation of our choices for good, it has the power to repair past injustices.

אִם יָרְדוּ יְחִידִים מֵהָאֻמָּה מִמַּדְרֵגַת-הַחַיִּים, הַמְּלֵאִים אוֹר-
קֹדֶשׁ וָחֹפֶשׁ, וְיֵעָשׂוּ לַעֲבָדִים בְּשָׁכְחָם אֶת עֶרְכָּם הָאֲצִילִי, וְ"אֹזֶן
שֶׁשָּׁמְעָה עַל הַר סִינַי: 'כִּי לִי בְּנֵי יִשְׂרָאֵל עֲבָדִים, עֲבָדַי הֵם וְלֹא
עֲבָדִים לַעֲבָדִים' – וְהָלַךְ זֶה וְקָנָה אָדוֹן לְעַצְמוֹ," הִנֵּה בָּאָה הַשַּׁבָּת
הַכָּבוֹד הָאִישִׁי וְחֵרוּתוֹ, מִתּוֹךְ זֶרֶם-חַיִּים שֶׁל קְדֻשַּׁת עֶלְיוֹן הַשּׁוֹפֵעַ
מֵהַמָּקוֹר הַיּוֹתֵר עֶלְיוֹן, שֶׁמִּמֶּנּוּ הָאֻמָּה יוֹנֶקֶת אֶת אוֹר נִשְׁמָתָהּ, -
וּדְרוֹר נִקְרָא בָּאָרֶץ לְכָל יוֹשְׁבֶיהָ. וּלְעֻמַּת אִי-שִׁוְיוֹן-הַמִּשְׁקָל שֶׁל
מַצַּב הָרְכוּשׁ הַקַּרְקָעִי, שֶׁהוּא בָּא מֵרִפְיוֹן יָדַיִם וְרוּחַ מִכָּל חַטֹּאת
הָאָדָם, הַמַּכְשִׁילוֹת אֶת כֹּחוֹ, עַד שֶׁהוּא יוֹרֵד מִנַּחֲלַת אֲבוֹתָיו, - בָּאָה
הַשַּׁבָּת, הַמַּתְאֶמֶת כְּפִי עֶרְכָּהּ שֶׁל הָאֻמָּה בְּרֵאשִׁית מַטָּעָהּ, בָּרְכוּשׁ
הַיְסוֹדִי הַזֶּה לְאוֹתָם אֲשֶׁר הִכְבִּידָה עֲלֵיהֶם תִּגְרַת הַחַיִּים וַתַּעֲוֵת אֶת
מִשְׁקָלָם, "בִּשְׁנַת-הַיּוֹבֵל הַזֹּאת תָּשֻׁבוּ אִישׁ אֶל-אֲחֻזָּתוֹ."

וְדַוְקָא בִּתְעוּפָה מְלֵאָה חַיִּים כְּמוֹ אֵלֶּה מִתְרוֹמֶמֶת הָאֻמָּה לְרָכֵּס
אֶת חַיֶּיהָ עִם חַיֵּי הָאָדָם בִּכְלָלוֹ, עַ"יْ אֶמְצָעוּתָם שֶׁל אִישִׁים יְחִידִים
– הַגֵּרִים הַתּוֹשָׁבִים – הָעוֹמְדִים בִּכְלָלוּתָם בְּתוֹךְ הָאֱנוֹשִׁיּוּת

---

32. Lev. 25:55.

33. Talmud Bavli, Kiddushin 22b. The Talmud here censures the Hebrew slave referred to in Exod. 21:6, who elects to remain a slave beyond the mandatory period. His choice shows that he has not internalized the innate freedom and dignity that attaches to being a servant of God, not of man. Rav Kook understands the return of each person to his ancestral land as the remedy for the indignity of selling oneself as a slave.

If individuals fall from the status of free men and women and, forgetting their inherent nobility, are made into servants—"the ear that heard the words at Sinai, 'the children of Israel are My servants'[32]—*My servants, and not the servants of My servants*"—and yet in spite of this he went and acquired a human master for himself[33]—now his freedom and self-respect are returned to him. Holiness flows into our lives from the highest source, the place from which the nation's soul suckles light and "freedom is proclaimed throughout the land to all its inhabitants."[34] Inequality in landed property, which resulted from bodily and spiritual weakness and error, sapped his strength, until he was forced to sell his ancestral patrimony. Now, however, restitution comes, corresponding to the people's status at the beginning of its journey. The original property returns to those who have suffered from the vicissitudes of life, distorting their sense of their true value: "In this Jubilee, everyone shall return to his original holdings."[35]

Such life-affirming flights of possibility will raise the people up to bind its life together with that of all humanity through those special people, the *gerim toshavim*—non-Jews who stand fully in the mainstream

34. Lev. 25:10.

35. Lev. 25:13.

הַכְּלָלִית וּמַרְגִּישִׁים בְּקִרְבָּם גַּם-כֵּן יַחַשׁ מְיֻחָד אֶל נְטִיּוֹתֶיהָ
הָרַעֲנַנּוֹת וּשְׁאִיפוֹתֶיהָ הָרוּחָנִיּוֹת שֶׁל הָאֻמָּה, וְדַוְקָא אָז מִתְכַּנֶּסֶת
בָּהּ הַתַּקִּיפוּת הַפְּנִימִית לִדְחוֹק אֶת הַחֵלֶק הַסִּיגִי שֶׁבְּעַצְמָהּ, כְּדֵי
שֶׁיָּאִיר יָפֶה הַמָּאוֹר הַכְּלָלִי הַמַּבְהִיק. "אֵין עֶבֶד עִבְרִי נוֹהֵג וְלֹא גֵר
תּוֹשָׁב נוֹהֵג אֶלָּא בִּזְמַן שֶׁהַיּוֹבֵל נוֹהֵג" (ערכין).

כָּל אֵלֶּה יַחַד הֵם סִימָנֵי-חַיִּים עֶלְיוֹנִים, שֶׁצְּרִיכָה לְגִלּוּיָתָם אֻמָּה זוֹ,
שֶׁמּוּסָר-לְאֻמִּי אֱלֹהִי כָּזֶה חַי בְּקִרְבָּהּ, וְנָכוֹן הוּא לְפָנֶיהָ, בִּהְיוֹתָהּ
מְבֻנָּה בְּכָל תַּכְסִיסֶיהָ בְּרוּם עִלּוּיֶהָ הַמְּדִינִי "כְּשֶׁכָּל יוֹשְׁבֶיהָ עָלֶיהָ,"
– לְמַעַן יַעֲלֶה בְּיָדָהּ תַּכְסִיס הִתְגַּלּוּת הַהַכָּרָה שֶׁל הַיֹּשֶׁר הָאֱלֹהִי,
הָעוֹמֵד לְמַעֲלָה מִסְּגֻלָּתָהּ הַמּוּכָנָה עִמָּהּ מִכְּבָר, הַשּׁוֹמֶרֶת עַל
תַּפְקִידֶיהָ שֶׁלֹּא יֵרְדוּ וְלֹא יִמָּחוּ כָּלִיל.

36. Talmud Bavli, Arakhin 29a. See the introduction to this volume for a short
     discussion of how Rav Kook reads this talmudic passage and the universal
     aspects of the Jubilee.

37. Talmud Bavli, Arakhin 32b. The Talmud sets "when all its inhabitants are liv-
     ing there" as a condition for the observance of the Jubilee year. This is inferred
     from the verse referring to the Jubilee "freedom is proclaimed throughout
     the land to *all its inhabitants*" (Lev. 25:10), i.e., the Jubilee's proclamation of
     freedom may occur only when all the land's inhabitants are living on it. Rav
     Kook understands that the fulfillment of this condition effects a qualitative
     change in the people's political situation.

of universal humanity and who also feel a special connection to the reinvigorated spiritual aspirations of the Jewish people; then there will arise an inner urge in the people to rein in the separatist element within itself so as to properly highlight the brilliant illumination of the universal: "The law of a Hebrew servant and the law of the *ger toshav* operate only when the Jubilee operates."[36]

All these are signs of a spiritual vitality that this people will manifest when a divine sense of morality is alive within them. They will emerge from the complexity of the nation's political situation in its full richness, "when all its inhabitants are living there."[37] Thus will the people find a way to reveal an awareness of the godly integrity that stands above its innate quality, that is already within it, and that protects the people's purposes so that they do not decline or disappear entirely.

כְּשֶׁהַבְּחִירָה הַמְקֻלְקֶלֶת מַשְׁקַעַת אֶת אוֹר עִלּוּי הַחַיִּים שֶׁל
"רְחוֹבוֹת־הַנָּהָר," הַהוֹלֵךְ וּמִשְׁתַּפֵּךְ גַּם מֵעַל לִגְבוּל יִשְׂרָאֵל, הִיא
פּוֹגֶמֶת אֶת יְסוֹד הַסְּגֻלָּה הַטִּבְעִית. אִי־אֶפְשָׁר לָהּ אָמְנָם לְהַכְחִידָה,
אֲבָל בְּיָדָהּ לְהַשְׁקִיעָהּ בְּמַעֲמַקִּים, עָמוֹק־עָמוֹק, עַד אֲשֶׁר תַּעֲלֹם
זְמַן רַב, עִדָּן וְעִדָּנִים, וְהָעָם יְקַו לָאוֹר וָאַיִן, עַד בֹּא עֵת־קֵץ.

הַתּוֹרָה, בְּדֵעוֹתֶיהָ חֻקֶּיהָ וּמִשְׁפָּטֶיהָ, לְחַיֵּי הַיָּחִיד וְהַצִּבּוּר, הִיא
הָאַסְפַּקְלַרְיָא הַמְּאִירָה, שֶׁבְּתוֹכָהּ מִשְׁתַּקֶּפֶת כָּל מַעֲלַת רוּחַ
הָאֻמָּה, בֵּין הָרוּחַ הַסְּגֻלִּי הַטִּבְעִי שֶׁל הַשְּׁמִטָּה וּבֵין רוּחַ עֶלְיוֹן רוּחַ
אֱלֹהִים־חַיִּים שֶׁל הַיּוֹבֵל, הַמִּתְגַּלֶּה בְּהִתְגַּלּוּתָהּ הַבְּחִירִית. כָּל־זְמַן
שֶׁהִיא מִשְׁתַּמֶּרֶת, בְּרוּחָהּ וּבְפָעֳלֶיהָ, בְּתוֹךְ הָאֻמָּה וְהָאָרֶץ וְסִדְרֵי־
הַחֶבְרָה, הֲרֵי הִיא נוֹתֶנֶת עֹז וְתַעֲצוּמוֹת לָעָם. הַדְּבֵקוּת־בֵּאלֹהִים
הָרַעֲנַנָּה מְשַׁעֲשַׁעַת הִיא אָז אֶת נִשְׁמַת־הַחַיִּים שֶׁלּוֹ וּמְרַעֲנֶנֶת אֶת
הַלֵּב שֶׁל כָּל פְּרָט. הִיא הוֹלֶכֶת וְזוֹרֶמֶת עַל אוֹר הָאֱמוּנָה הָאֱלֹהִית
עַ"פ הַכָּרָתָהּ שֶׁל הָאֻמָּה מִצַּד נִשְׁמַת סְגֻלָּתָהּ הַטִּבְעִית, אֲשֶׁר
בֵּירוּרֶיהָ הַתּוֹלְדָתִּיִּים שֶׁהִיא מְעֻטֶּרֶת בָּהֶם, בְּנוֹזְרֵי יְשׁוּעָה מִדּוֹר־
דּוֹרִים, הֵם מַכְשִׁירִים אֶת הַכָּרָתָהּ הָאֱלֹהִית הַמְיֻחֶדֶת לְפִי צִבְיוֹנָהּ

---

38. Hebrew, *rehovot hanahar*: a kabbalistic term based on Gen. 36:37, meaning
the broadening of wisdom. Rabbi Schneur Zalman of Liadi, the founder of
Chabad, characterizes *rehovot hanahar* as the spreading of the kabbalistic *sefira* of *ḥokhma* (wisdom), which he likens to a wellspring, into the *sefira* of *bina*
(intellect), which he compares to a river (*Likutei Torah, Shir hashirim* 39b).

When corrupted choice darkens the light of the life of "broad spaces by the river,"[38] which grows and overspills the borders of Israel, such choice mars the foundation of Israel's natural excellence—though it cannot destroy it. But it can plunge that treasure deep, deep down into the depths, until it disappears for a long time, eons and eons. The people will long for light, when there is none, until the time of the End.

The Torah, with its ideas, statutes, and laws, for the life of the individual and the community, is a clear glass, in which all the spiritual qualities of the people are reflected—whether the natural, intrinsic impulses that are expressed in observance of shmita, or the higher, divine spirit of the Jubilee, which is manifested through the people's choices. So long as the Torah is observed, both in letter and in spirit, in the people, the land, and in the way society is ordered, it gives strength to the nation. The reenergizing closeness to God will then thrill the life soul of the people and bring joy to the heart of each individual. The light of faith will stream through the consciousness of the people from its natural, distinctive spirit; the refinements of this spirit that take place generation by generation will adorn the people, dedicated, as they are, to salvation from time immemorial, and these refinements will train the people's unique, divine consciousness according to its individual character. This distinctive

הַפְּרָטִי. וְהַהַכָּרָה הַמְיֻחֶדֶת הַזּוֹ הוֹלֶכֶת וּפוֹעֶלֶת וְחוֹזֶרֶת וּמִתְפַּעֶלֶת מֵהַטּוֹב הַכְּלָלִי שֶׁל אוֹר אֱלֹהִים, שֶׁבָּאָדָם וּבָעוֹלָם, הִיא מְטִיבָה אוֹתוֹ, מְסַגֶּלֶת אוֹתוֹ אֵלֶיהָ בְּהַטְבִּיעָה בּוֹ אֶת צִבְיוֹנָהּ הַפְּרָטִי, וּמַכְשִׁירָתוֹ בָּזֶה לְמַלֵּא חַדְרֵי כָל רוּחַ וָנֶפֶשׁ בְּרִגְשֵׁי-טֹהַר וְחֶדְוַת-יֹשֶׁר הַמְבֻסָּסִים בְּנִצְחִיּוּתָם בְּעֶדְנָם הָאֱלֹהִי, שֶׁהוּא מַצִּילָם מִכָּל יֵאוּשׁ וּמִשַּׂגְּבֵם יֶשַׁע עֲדֵי עַד.

עוֹלָה הִיא הָאֻמָּה בְּרוּם מַעֲלוֹתֶיהָ אֵלֶּה – כְּשֶׁהִיא מַכֶּרֶת אֶת רוּחָהּ הָעַצְמִי. הַכָּרָה זוֹ הִיא מְבִיאָה אוֹתָהּ לְהֵעָטֵר בְּגֹדֶל לֵבָב בְּתוֹרַת-אֱלֹהִים אֲשֶׁר עֻמָּדָהּ, הִיא מַרְכִּבָתָהּ עַל בָּמֳתֵי אָרֶץ. וְעַד כַּמָּה שֶׁיִּהְיוּ חַיֵּי כָל הַסְּבִיבָה כֻּלָּהּ בִּלְתִּי-מֻכְשָׁרִים אוֹ מְנֻגָּדִים לְאוֹתָהּ הָרוֹמְמוּת הָאֱלֹהִית, שֶׁרוּחַ יִשְׂרָאֵל שׁוֹאֵף אֵלֶיהָ, לֹא תֵּלֵךְ בְּמִצוּדָתָם, וְאֶת דַּרְכָּהּ תֵּלֵךְ לָבֶטַח. אָז תְּעוֹרֵר אֶת סְגֻלַּת-טִבְעָהּ וְאֶת הַהוֹד חֵיל בְּחִירָתָהּ אַחֲרֶיהָ. הַשְּׁמִטָּה וְהַיּוֹבֵל יַחְדָּו יִהְיוּ תַמִּים עַל רֹאשָׁהּ וְהָאָרֶץ תַּעֲנֶה לְעֻמָּתָהּ בְּחֵילָהּ הָרוּחָנִי הָאָצוּר בְּקִרְבָּהּ, הַמַּתְאִים לְחֶדְוַת הַשְּׁמִטָּה וְרִנְנַת הַיּוֹבֵל. "וְצִוִּיתִי אֶת-בִּרְכָתִי לָכֶם בַּשָּׁנָה הַשִּׁשִּׁית וְעָשָׂת אֶת-הַתְּבוּאָה לִשְׁלֹשׁ הַשָּׁנִים." "יִרְעֲפוּ נְאוֹת מִדְבָּר וְגִיל גְּבָעוֹת תַּחְגֹּרְנָה." "לָבְשׁוּ כָרִים הַצֹּאן וַעֲמָקִים יַעַטְפוּ בָר יִתְרוֹעֲעוּ אַף יָשִׁירוּ."

---

39. The second half of this paragraph is especially unclear.

40. Lev. 25:21. The verse promises God's blessing on the sixth year so that the shmita will not cause shortage or hardship.

awareness will continually do its work, and will in turn be worked upon by the universal good of divine light. This light sharpens our awareness and stamps upon it its particular form, enabling it to fill up all the recesses of spirit and soul with pure feelings and upright joy, which are founded eternally on divine delight, which saves one from all despair and raises up everlasting salvation.[39]

The people rises to these levels when it knows its own particular spirit. This self-knowledge allows the people to be crowned with the divine Torah that stands at the summit of the world. However inhospitable, or even hostile, the surroundings are to the godly heights for which Israel yearns, she will not be caught in their snares but will go confidently on her way. Then her natural inner character and the splendor of her power of moral choice will be awakened. The shmita and the Jubilee will adorn her, and the land will respond to the people, with all the spiritual goodness that is within her, attuned to the joy of shmita and the Jubilee. "I will ordain my blessing for you in the sixth year so that it shall yield a crop sufficient for three years."[40] "The pasturelands distill it; the hills are girded with joy. The meadows are clothed with flocks, the valleys mantled with grain; they raise a shout, they break into song."[41]

41. Ps. 65:13–14. The antecedent of "it" in the previous verse (65:12) is "God's bounty." Rav Kook cites this verse as an image of blessing and plenty.

כְּשֶׁעָמְמָה בְּיִשְׂרָאֵל הַכָּרַת הָרוּחַ הָעַצְמִי "זָנַח יִשְׂרָאֵל טוֹב," שָׁכַח
אֶת עֻזּוֹ וְגַאֲוָתוֹ. הַמַּבָּט הַחִיצוֹנִי עַל הַסְּבִיבָה הָרְחָבָה הַבִּלְתִּי-
מְפֻתַּחַת, הַפְּרָאִית בְּטִבְעָהּ וּבְבְחִירָתָהּ גַּם יַחַד, הִשְׁכִּיחַ מִמֶּנּוּ אֶת
גַּדְלַת סְגֻלָּתוֹ. אָז הָסְעוּ מִן הַלֵּב תְּשׁוּקַת הַחַיִּים הָאֱלֹהִיִּים וְעֶדְנֵיהֶם
וְחֶמְדַּת מְשׁוֹשָׁם וְחֵילָם בְּהִתְגַּלְמָם בְּפֹעַל, בְּאֶרֶץ-הַחַיִּים. טָהֳרַת
הַשֵּׂכֶל הַפָּשׁוּט וְהַבָּרוּר הַשְּׁבָתָהּ, זִיו הַצֶּדֶק הוּעַם. אֶת עֶמְדָּתָם
לָקְחוּ הַדִּמְיוֹן הַגַּס שֶׁל הַחֶבְרָה הַפְּרוּעָה וְרֶשַׁע-כֶּסֶל שֶׁל הַהֲזָיוֹת
הָאֱלִילִיּוֹת וְתוֹעֲבוֹתֵיהֶן. בְּמַשְּׂאוֹן כָּסְתָה הַסְּגֻלָּה הָאֱלֹהִית הָאֲצוּלָה
בְּנִשְׁמַת הָאֻמָּה וְלֹא תוּכַל עוֹד לָקַחַת לֵב חֶמְדַּת חַיֵּי טֹהַר, שֶׁקֶט
וָיֹשֶׁר. תְּכוּנַת הָאֻמָּה בְּרִדְתָּהּ הוֹסִיפָה יְרִידָה גַּם לִתְכוּנַת רוּחַ הָאָרֶץ
שֶׁהוּא מַתְאִים עִמָּהּ הַתְאָמָה נִצַּחַת: בְּחֻלְשַׁת נִשְׁמַת הָאֻמָּה לֹא
תִּתֵּן סְגֻלַּת הָאָרֶץ אֶת תַּפְקִידָהּ. רוּחַ הָאָרֶץ, רוּחַ אֶרֶץ חֶמְדָּה
הַמְּלֵאָה שִׁירַת-קֹדֶשׁ וְרִנְנַת-יָהּ, יָרַד מַטָּה-מַטָּה. "וַתֶּחֱטָא הָאָרֶץ
וָאֶפְקֹד עֲוֹנָהּ עָלֶיהָ וַתָּקִא הָאָרֶץ אֶת יֹשְׁבֶיהָ." רוּחַ הָאֻמָּה בְּכְלָלָהּ
סָפַג אֶל תּוֹכוֹ יְסוֹדוֹת רָעִים וְזָרִים, עַד אֲשֶׁר הֶעֱיב אֶת טָהֳרָתוֹ

---

42. Hosea 8:3. See also *Orot hakodesh*, 3:140, where Rav Kook cites the same biblical verse to connote the spurning—by the individual or community—of one's unique, divine source of being.

When Israel's awareness of its own spirit became foggy—"Israel rejects what is good"[42]—the people forgot its strength and pride. Looking superficially at their undeveloped and wild environment made them forget their inner greatness. The yearning for a refined, godly life slipped from their hearts, as did the sense of joyful strength that one has when life is clothed in deeds. Clear, simple, pure-hearted understanding ceased, and the light of justice was dimmed. In its place came the coarse imagination of a lawless society, and the dumb, evil delusions of idolatry, with all its attendant abominations. Under their burden, the sublime, divine character of the people was smothered, and there were no more pure, upright, and serene hearts. This moral collapse in the nation was matched by a decline in the spiritual character of the land, which had always been intertwined with the moral life of the people. As the people became spiritually weaker, the special qualities of the land could no longer find fulfillment. The spirit of the precious land, full of holy song and godly gladness, plummeted. "Thus the land became defiled; and I called it to account for its iniquity, and the land spewed out its inhabitants."[43] The people absorbed bad influences, which coarsened its pure nature.

43. Lev. 18:25.

הָעַצְמָאִית. "כִּי זָנְתָה אִמָּם הֹבִישָׁה הוֹרָתָם." אַף בְּכָל הַצִּיּוּרִים
הַיּוֹתֵר קְדוֹשִׁים, הַחֲתוּמִים בְּאָפְיָהּ שֶׁל הָאֻמָּה, הֻטַּל הָרַעַל,
"חָדְשֵׁיכֶם וּמוֹעֲדֵיכֶם שָׂנְאָה נַפְשִׁי הָיוּ עָלַי לָטֹרַח נִלְאֵיתִי נְשֹׂא."
וְהַחַיִּים הַלְּאֻמִּיִּים, אַחֲרֵי אֲשֶׁר הִטַּמְּאוּ, הוֹסִיפוּ לָהּ חֳלָיִים מוּסָרִיִּים
כַּבִּירִים, וַיִּהְיוּ עִם שְׁאוֹנָם הַמְּדִינִי רַק לִמְהוּמָה פְּנִימִית הַמְּהַמְמֶת
אֶת הַנֶּפֶשׁ. שְׁנֵי הַיְסוֹדוֹת, הָאֻמָּה וְהָאָרֶץ, אֲשֶׁר בִּבְרִיאוּתָם הֵם
מוֹסִיפִים זֶה לָזֶה כָּל-כָּךְ לְוָיַת-חֵן, כָּל-כָּךְ אֹמֶץ וָעֹז, הֶחֵלוּ מַשְׁפִּיעִים
זֶה לָזֶה בַּחֲלוֹתָם – לְרָעָה וְלִזְוָעָה, עַד אֲשֶׁר הֻכְרְחָה לָקַחַת מַעֲמַד
הָרְפוּאָה הָרַחֲמָנִית-הָאַכְזָרִיָּה, הַנִּתּוּחַ הַנּוֹרָא, הִתְרַחֲקוּת הָאֻמָּה
מֵהָאָרֶץ "וּמִפְּנֵי חֲטָאֵינוּ גָּלִינוּ מֵאַרְצֵנוּ וְנִתְרַחַקְנוּ מֵעַל אַדְמָתֵנוּ."
בְּעֶצֶם צָרָתָהּ הַגְּדוֹלָה שֶׁל הָאֻמָּה, כַּאֲשֶׁר סָר מִקִּרְבָּהּ שְׁאוֹנָם שֶׁל
הַחַיִּים הַלְּאֻמִּיִּים וּמְהוּמָתָם הַמְּזֶקֶת, הֵחֵל הָאוֹר הָרוּחָנִי לָשׁוּב
לַעֲלוֹת לְאִטּוֹ בְּקִרְבָּהּ בַּמַּעֲלוֹת אֲשֶׁר יָרַד. רוּחַ הָאֻמָּה הוֹסִיף

---

44. Hosea 2:7. The prophet compares Israel's pursuit of idolatry to an adulterous woman's pursuit of lovers.

45. Isa. 1:7. In this passage, God rejects the people's ritual worship when their moral life is full of oppression and cruelty.

46. This statement might appear paradoxical in the context of a passage about the moral collapse of the people. The meaning appears to be that, with the decline of the national, political life of the Jewish people, there were outbursts of moral intensity, but these were unsustainable in the absence of supporting political institutions. Rav Kook may have been thinking of a phenomenon analogous to the proliferation of ascetic Jewish sects toward the end of the Second Temple period.

"In that their mother has played the harlot, she that conceived them has acted shamelessly."[44] Even the most holy images engraved on the face of the people became toxic: "Your new moons and fixed seasons fill me with loathing. They have become a burden to me, and I cannot endure them."[45] When national life became defiled, the power of ethics increased,[46] but with the surrounding political turmoil, the result was simply inner anguish and confusion. These two elements—the people and the land, which, when healthy, had given each other so much grace and power for good—made each other sicker and more corrupt. Finally, they had to take the cruel-kind medicine, the dreadful surgical operation of separating the people from the land—"Because of our sins, we were exiled from our country and distanced from our land."[47]

From deep within the people's terrible troubles, after their turbulent national life with all its destructive turmoil had been taken away from them, their spiritual light and strength began gradually to return to the levels from which it had declined. The people's spirit began to soar

47. Taken from the *musaf* prayer for the new moon and festivals.

לְהַעֲלוֹת-אֵבֶר כְּפִי מִדַּת שְׁבִיתָתוֹ מֵהַחַיִּים הַמְדִינִיִּים, שֶׁהֵם
רִאשׁוֹנִים לְטֻמְאָה בְּצִבּוּר מְקֻלְקָל. "וָאֹמַר אֵלֶיהָ יָמִים רַבִּים תֵּשְׁבִי
לִי לֹא תִזְנִי וְלֹא תִהְיִי לְאִישׁ וְגַם אֲנִי אֵלָיִךְ. כִּי יָמִים רַבִּים יֵשְׁבוּ בְּנֵי
יִשְׂרָאֵל אֵין מֶלֶךְ וְאֵין שָׂר וְאֵין זֶבַח וְאֵין מַצֵּבָה וְאֵין אֵפוֹד וּתְרָפִים."
"וְהָיָה בַיּוֹם הַהוּא נְאֻם יְהֹוָה וְהִכְרַתִּי סוּסֶיךָ מִקִּרְבֶּךָ וְהַאֲבַדְתִּי
מַרְכְּבֹתֶיךָ, וְהִכְרַתִּי עָרֵי אַרְצֶךָ וְהָרַסְתִּי כָּל מִבְצָרֶיךָ. וְהִכְרַתִּי
כְשָׁפִים מִיָּדֶךָ וּמְעוֹנְנִים לֹא יִהְיוּ לָךְ. וְהִכְרַתִּי פְסִילֶיךָ וּמַצֵּבוֹתֶיךָ
מִקִּרְבֶּךָ וְלֹא תִשְׁתַּחֲוֶה עוֹד לְמַעֲשֵׂה יָדֶיךָ."

"וַהֲשִׁמֹּתִי אֲנִי אֶת הָאָרֶץ וְשָׁמְמוּ עָלֶיהָ אֹיְבֵיכֶם הַיֹּשְׁבִים בָּהּ.
וְאֶתְכֶם אֱזָרֶה בַגּוֹיִם וַהֲרִיקֹתִי אַחֲרֵיכֶם חָרֶב וְהָיְתָה אַרְצְכֶם שְׁמָמָה
וְעָרֵיכֶם יִהְיוּ חָרְבָּה. אָז תִּרְצֶה הָאָרֶץ אֶת שַׁבְּתֹתֶיהָ כֹּל יְמֵי הָשַּׁמָּה
וְאַתֶּם בְּאֶרֶץ אֹיְבֵיכֶם אָז תִּשְׁבַּת הָאָרֶץ וְהִרְצָת אֶת שַׁבְּתֹתֶיהָ. כָּל
יְמֵי הֳשַּׁמָּה תִּשְׁבֹּת אֵת אֲשֶׁר לֹא שָׁבְתָה בְּשַׁבְּתֹתֵיכֶם בְּשִׁבְתְּכֶם

---

48. Hosea 3:2. In this passage, the betrayed husband takes back his previously unfaithful wife, giving her merely "fifteen pieces of silver, a *homer* of barley, and a *letekh* of barley." Similarly, God resumes his intimacy with the Jewish people but removes from them the trappings of national sovereignty, which had aided their betrayal.

49. Mic. 5:9–12.

50. Lev. 26:32–35. These verses imply that exile was the punishment for not observing shmita; during the years of dispersion, the land will make up for the sabbaticals that were not properly kept while the Jewish people dwelled in the land.

again, the longer they were separated from politics and statecraft—which are poisonous to a broken society. "I stipulated with her: in return, you will go a long time without either fornicating or marrying; even I shall not cohabit with you. For the Israelites shall go a long time without king and without officials, without sacrifice and without cult pillars and without ephod and teraphim."[48] "In that day, I will destroy the horses in your midst and wreck your chariots. I will destroy the cities of your land and demolish all your fortresses. I will destroy the sorcery you practice, and you shall have no more soothsayers. I will destroy your idols and the sacred pillars in your midst; and no more shall you bow down to the work of your hands."[49]

"I will make the land desolate, so that your enemies who settle in it shall be appalled by it. And you, I will scatter among the nations, and I will unsheathe the sword against you. Your land shall become a desolation and your cities a ruin. Then shall the land make up for its Sabbath years, throughout the time that it is desolate and you are in the land of your enemies; then shall the land rest and make up for its Sabbath years. Throughout the time that it is desolate, it shall observe the rest that it did not observe in your Sabbath years while you were dwelling upon it."[50]

עָלֶיהָ. "וְהָאָרֶץ תֵּעָזֵב מֵהֶם וְתִרֶץ אֶת שַׁבְּתֹתֶיהָ בָּהְשַׁמָּה מֵהֶם וְהֵם יִרְצוּ אֶת עֲוֹנָם יַעַן וּבְיַעַן בְּמִשְׁפָּטַי מָאָסוּ וְאֶת חֻקֹּתַי גָּעֲלָה נַפְשָׁם."

יִשְׂרָאֵל בְּגוֹלָה עָזַב אֶת דַּאֲגָתוֹ מִכָּל עִנְיְנֵי-חוֹל מִצַּד כְּלָלוּת הָאֻמָּה. שָׁם אֶת עֵינָיו וְלִבּוֹ רַק בַּשָּׁמַיִם מִמַּעַל. לִבּוֹ לֹא הָלַךְ עוֹד לְהַרְבּוֹת חֵיל רֶכֶב וָסוּס, כְּכָל גּוֹי עַל אַדְמָתוֹ. וּבִכְלָל לֹא הָיָה עוֹד לְכְלָל הָאֻמָּה שׁוּם עֵסֶק חָמְרִי. יַחַד עִם זֶה חָדַל לַעֲגֹב אֶל כָּל תַּזְנוּנֵי הַגּוֹיִם הָרַבִּים. וְרוּחַ-ד' הֵחֵל לְפַעֲמוֹ לְהַשְׂכִּיל אֶל עֵרֶךְ הָאָדָם וּמַעֲלַת נִשְׁמָתוֹ, וְכֵן לְהוֹקִיר בְּיִחוּד אֶת עֶרְכָּהּ הָרוּחָנִי שֶׁל הָאֻמָּה וְיִתְרוֹנָהּ הָאֱלֹהִי. הַתּוֹרָה נִתְחַבְּבָה עָלָיו מִזָּהָב וּמִפָּז רַב כִּבִּימֵי-נְעוּרָיו הַטּוֹבִים. עַל קְדֻשַּׁת הָאֱמוּנָה וְהַמִּצְוֹת יָצָא לַהוֹרֵג בְּשִׂמְחַת-לֵבָב. עֵינָיו וְלִבּוֹ, אֲשֶׁר הָיוּ בַּשָּׁמַיִם תָּמִיד, הֶעֱלוּ אֲרוּכָה לְכָל מְשׁוּבוֹת הַחַיִּים הַלְּאֻמִּיִּים וּלְכָל פִּשְׁעֵיהֶם, וּמֵעֵת אֲשֶׁר הִתְרַחֵק מֵאַרְצוֹ פָּנָה תָּמִיד אֵלֶיהָ, - אֲבָל לֹא בְּמַבָּט גַּס, לֹא כְּכָל שׁוֹכֵן-בֵּית-חֹמֶר

51. Lev. 26:43.
52. Ps. 19:11.
53. See Jer. 8:22.

"For the land shall be forsaken of them, making up for its Sabbath years by being desolate of them, while they atone for their iniquity; for the abundant reason that they rejected My rules and spurned My laws."[51]

In exile, Israel abandoned its preoccupation with secular matters that concerned the people as a whole, and turned its eyes and hearts toward heaven. It stopped trying to amass power, chariots, and horses like every other people on earth, and the nation as a collective ceased all materialist pursuits. It no longer desired the debaucheries of the surrounding peoples. The spirit of God began to beat within the people once again and to awaken them to know the true heights of the human soul. So, too, they became aware once more of the Jewish people's spiritual potential. The Torah became more precious to them "than gold, than much fine gold,"[52] as it had been in the good times of the people's youth. They were willing to accept death joyfully for the sake of their holy faith and commandments. Their eyes and hearts, which were habitually cast heavenward, began to recuperate[53] from the backslidings and sins of their national life. From the time they were separated from the land, they turned toward it—not with the greedy gaze of one who sits in his

הַמִּשְׁתּוֹקֵק אֶל אֶרֶץ מְכוֹרָתוֹ מִפְּנֵי שֶׁהִיא מַשְׂבִּיעָתוֹ לֶחֶם וּמְסַפֶּקֶת
לוֹ אֶת חֲפָצָיו הַחָמְרִיִּים, כִּי בְּעֵינַיִם מְלֵאוֹת חִבַּת קֹדֶשׁ הִבִּיט אֵלֶיהָ,
אֶל סְגֻלָּתָהּ הַפְּנִימִית, הַמַּתְאִימָה לַתְּשׁוּקָה הָאֱלֹהִית אֲשֶׁר הֵחֵלָּה
לָשׁוּב לְתוֹכוֹ.

כֵּן הָאָרֶץ הִתְנַעֲרָה מִטֻּמְאָתָהּ. "שִׁכּוֹרֵי-אֶפְרַיִם," שָׂרִים סוֹרְרִים
וְחַבְרֵי גַּנָּבִים, אֹהֲבֵי שֹׁחַד וְרֹדְפֵי שַׁלְמוֹנִים, הַבּוֹעֲטִים מֵרֹב טוֹבָה,
נִמְחוּ מִמֶּנָּה יַחַד עִם כָּל חָסְנָהּ וְתִפְאַרְתָּהּ. אַחַר יָמִים רַבִּים הֵחֵלָּה,
אָמְנָם לִמְשֹׁךְ אֵלֶיהָ לְאַט לְאַט נִדָּחִים יְחִידִים, - אֲבָל רַק בְּכֹחַהּ
לֵאלֹהִים, בִּקְדֻשָּׁתָהּ הָעֶלְיוֹנָה הַמִּתְעַלָּה עַל כָּל חֵפֶץ חַיֵּי-חֹמֶר
וּדְרִישַׁת מִשְׂטְרֵי-לְאֹם.

54.   Isa. 28:1. The full verse reads: "Ah, the proud crowns of the drunkards of Ephraim, whose glorious beauty is but wilted flowers on the heads of men bloated with rich food, who are overcome with wine."

house and desires to reacquire the land that he had sold because it supplied him with bread and other physical needs, but rather with a look of holy love for its inner character, befitting the godly desire that had begun to return to the people.

So the land will shake off the impurity of the "drunkards of Ephraim"[54]—the rebellious rulers and gangs of thieves who love bribery and pursue only their own gain, kicking against God out of their abundance of good things. They will melt away, along with all their power and glory.

After a long time, scattered individuals gradually began returning to the land, drawn there by God's hand and by the holiness of the land rather than by any concern with material well-being or with reestablishing national government.[55]

---

55. Rav Kook refers to the trickle of pious individual Jews who found their way to the Land of Israel from the thirteenth century onward. In the early nineteenth century, the numbers of such immigrants increased, motivated by the messianic expectations directed to the 600th year of the sixth millennium (1840), based on prophecies of the Zohar. Between 1808 and 1840, the Jewish community in the Land of Israel more than doubled in size. The most notable group consisted of more than 500 disciples of the Gaon of Vilna, who arrived around 1813. See Arie Morgenstern, *Hastening Redemption: Messianism and the Resettlement of the Land of Israel* (Oxford: Oxford University Press, 2006), for an account of the fascinating and little-known episode of pre-Zionist Jewish immigration to Israel.

"קֵץ יְשׁוּעָה נִסְתַּם חָרַךְ. "לִבָּא לְפוּמָא לֹא גַּלְיָא." מִי בָּא בְּסוֹד ד'
לָדַעַת מָתַי הִטָּהֲרוּ כָּלִיל הָאָרֶץ וְהַגּוֹי מִטֻּמְאַת-הַנִּדָּה אֲשֶׁר לָהֶם,
מָתַי שָׁב הָרוּחַ, הַמִּסְתַּתֵּר בְּעַצְמוּתוֹ וְנִגְלָה בִּפְעֻלּוֹתָיו, כְּפִי מִדַּת
הַכְשָׁרַת הַמַּצָּבִים הַחִיצוֹנִים הַמַּכְשִׁירִים אֶת הִתְגַּלּוּתוֹ בָּאֻמָּה
וּבָאָרֶץ, - אֶל טַהֲרוֹ וְחָסְנוֹ, וּמָתַי הִגִּיעָה עֵת-דּוֹדִים, אֲשֶׁר בְּהִתְחַבֵּר
הָאֻמָּה וְהָאָרֶץ יַחַד יִפְעַל כָּל אֶחָד מֵהֶם עַל חֲבֵרוֹ לְטוֹבָה וְלִבְרָכָה,
וְלֹא כַּאֲשֶׁר הָיוּ בִּימֵי הַחֹשֶׁךְ, - אֵין אִתָּנוּ יוֹדֵעַ עַד-מָה. וּבְכֵן עֵינֵינוּ
נְשׂוּאוֹת לַחֲזוֹת אֶת חֶבְיוֹנֵי-הַמִּסְתָּרִים בִּמְקוֹם-רוֹאִים, - בַּחֲזוֹן
קֵץ הַמְגֻלֶּה, אֲשֶׁר חֲכָמִים מֵאָז הִבִּיעוּ: "אֵין לְךָ קֵץ מְגֻלֶּה מִזֶּה,
שֶׁנֶּאֱמַר: "וְאַתֶּם הָרֵי יִשְׂרָאֵל עַנְפְּכֶם תִּתֵּנוּ וּפֶרְיְכֶם תִּשְׂאוּ לְעַמִּי
יִשְׂרָאֵל כִּי קֵרְבוּ לָבוֹא." "וּפָנִיתִי אֲלֵיכֶם וְהִפְרֵיתִי אֶתְכֶם וְהִרְבֵּיתִי
אֶתְכֶם וַהֲקִימֹתִי אֶת-בְּרִיתִי אִתְּכֶם, וַעֲבַדְתֶּם וְנִזְרַעְתֶּם,
וְהִרְבֵּיתִי עֲלֵיכֶם אָדָם כָּל בֵּית יִשְׂרָאֵל כֻּלֹּה וְנֹשְׁבוּ הֶעָרִים וְהֶחֳרָבוֹת
תִּבָּנֶינָה, וְהִרְבֵּיתִי עֲלֵיכֶם אָדָם וּבְהֵמָה וְרָבוּ וּפָרוּ וְהוֹשַׁבְתִּי אֶתְכֶם
כְּקַדְמוֹתֵיכֶם וְהֵטִבֹתִי מֵרִאשֹׁתֵיכֶם וִידַעְתֶּם כִּי-אֲנִי ד'."

---

56. This appears to be a reference to Rashi's comment on Gen. 49:1: Jacob "wished to reveal the messianic end, but the divine presence was removed from him." See also Rashi's source, Genesis Raba 98:2.

57. Kohelet Raba 12:10.

58. Talmud Bavli, Sanhedrin 98a. See also Rashi ad loc. "When the Land of Israel generously gives of her fruits, then redemption is drawing near; there is no more obvious sign of the messianic end than this." Rav Kook urges paying attention to the renewed flourishing of agriculture in the Land of Israel as a portent of impending redemption.

"The appointed time of salvation is concealed."[56] "What is in the heart is not revealed to the mouth."[57] Who can know God's secrets and say precisely when the impurity of the land and the people will be lifted, when the spirit, hidden in its essence but revealed in its actions, will return once again in response to improvements in the outward situation that enable its reappearance in strength and purity upon the people and the land? When will the time of lovers come again, when the people and the land will reunite and mutual goodness and blessing will flow from their relationship—not like in the days of darkness? No one knows. So we raise our eyes to see the signs that are hidden in plain sight. In their vision of the messianic era, the sages said that "there is no messianic portent more obvious than this":[58] "But you, O mountains of Israel, shall yield your produce and bear your fruit for My people Israel, for their return is near. For I will care for you: I will turn to you, and you shall be tilled and sown. I will settle a large population on you, the whole house of Israel; the towns shall be resettled and the ruined sites rebuilt. I will multiply men and beasts upon you, and they shall increase and be fertile, and I will resettle you as you were formerly, and will make you more prosperous than you were at first. And you shall know that I am the Lord."[59]

59. Ezek. 36:8–11. This is the prooftext cited in Sanhedrin 98a (see n. 59 above).

כָּל עוֹד שֶׁלֹּא כָּלָה כָּלָה זַעַם, כָּל זְמַן שֶׁבְּמַעֲמַקֵּי רוּחַ הָאֻמָּה וְהָאָרֶץ לֹא
שָׁרָה עֲדַיִן חֶלְאָתָם מֵהֶם, הָיְתָה אָז כָּל סִבַּת פְּנוֹתָם רַק אֶל עַל, אֶל
קֹדֶשׁ ד', רַק מֵרֹב שׁוֹמְמוּתָם, מִפְּנֵי שֶׁלֹּא הָיָה לָהֶם כָּל עִנְיָן לָקַחַת
לֵב אָדָם הַחַי חַיֵּי חֹמֶר עֲלֵי אֲדָמוֹת: אֲבָל אִם יִתְגַּלּוּ אָז בְּחַיֵּי-חֶבְרָה
וּמִשְׁטַר-אָרֶץ, מִיָּד יִתְגַּלֶּה רוּחַ-הָעֲוֹעִים אֲשֶׁר בְּחֻכָּם וְהַהַשְׁחָתוֹת
הָעַתִּיקוֹת תָּשׁוּבְנָה וּתְקִיצֶינָה. בְּכֵן נִסְתַּם עַד אָז כָּל הֶחָזוֹן-רוּחַ,
הָאָרֶץ נִשְׁכְּחָה כָּמֵת מִלֵּב כְּלַל הָאֻמָּה, וְהַיְחִידִים, שֶׁעָלָה עַל לִבָּם
לִפְנוֹת אֵלֶיהָ, לֹא הָיָה לָהֶם כְּלָל שׁוּם עִנְיָן הַמִּתְיַחֵס לְצִדָּהּ הַחָמְרִי
הָאַרְצִי.

אֲבָל בְּמִדַּת הִתְמַלְּאוּת הַסְּאָה שֶׁל גַּעֲרַת ד' וְתוֹכַחְתּוֹ, שֶׁהִיא
מְרַקָּה לֹא רַק אֶת הַיְחִידִים, - שֶׁהֵם שָׁבוּ בְּרֻבָּם בִּימֵי-הַגָּלוּת
הָרִאשׁוֹנִים, - כִּי-אִם אֶת רוּחַ הָאֻמָּה בִּכְלָלָהּ, וַתְּרוֹמֵם אִתּוֹ יַחַד
אֶת רוּחַ הָאָרֶץ אֲשֶׁר נִשְׁפַּל בִּימֵי-הָרָעָה, - בְּמִדָּה זוֹ הֶחֵלּוּ דַּרְכֵי צִיּוֹן
הָאֲבֵלוֹת לְבַקֵּשׁ אֶת תַּפְקִידָן. הָעָם אֲשֶׁר נֶעֱזַב מֵהֶן הֵחֵל לַחֲשׁוֹב
עַל דְּבַר חֵפֶץ שׁוּבוֹ אֶל עָרָיו וְאֶל אַרְצוֹ, לִמְצֹא שָׁמָּה חַיִּים שְׁלֵמִים,
חַיִּים הַמְמַלְּאִים אֶת כָּל הַפְּגוּם מִצַּד הַחֹמֶר וְהָרוּחַ, גַּם יַחַד. רַק
זֶה מִקָּרוֹב הֵחֵל הָרוּחַ לְפַעַם, בְּמִסְתָּרִים בָּא, עוֹד סֵתֶר-פָּנִים לוֹ,
מְיֻדָּעָיו הָרַבִּים לֹא יוּכְלוּ לְהַכִּירוֹ וְיוֹדְעָיו לֹא חָזוּ יָמָיו. אַף אִם נִרְאָה
מֵרֵאשִׁית צְמִיחָתוֹ בַּחֲזוֹן-לֵב לִקְדוֹשֵׁי-רוּחַ, - רְאוּהוּ וְלֹא הִכִּירוּהוּ

---

60. Job 24:1.

So long as the anger has not been assuaged, and so long as the sickness in the depths of the people's soul has not been fully cured, there was every reason for them to turn only to heaven for support. Because of the extent of the land's destruction, people were not interested in trying to live a life closely tied to the earth; if dreams of restoring political sovereignty had occurred to them then, their confusions and ancient corruptions would likely have been to return and reawaken. So their spiritual vision was blocked, and most people forgot about the land, and the scattered individuals who were concerned with it related to it as a spiritual ideal rather than as a physical reality.

But with the fulfillment of the whole measure of God's rebuke (which refines not just individuals, who began to return from the early days of the exile, but also the spirit of the nation as a whole, which lifts up with it the degraded spirit of the land), the mourning for Zion began to seek outlets in action. The people that felt itself abandoned by Zion began to conceive the desire to return to its city and its land, to find there a life that would be more whole, in which the spiritual and physical could be healed simultaneously. Then the spirit began secretly to beat again, imperceptibly to most people—"Even those close to Him cannot foresee His actions."[60] Even if this initial growth was apparent to those with seeing

בְּעֻזּוֹ וּמַמָּשׁוּתוֹ, עַד אֲשֶׁר בְּמִסְבּוֹת הִתְהַפֵּךְ וְהִנֵּהוּ הוֹלֵךְ וְנִגְלֶה. הַשְּׁדֵרוֹת הַקְּרוֹבוֹת יוֹתֵר לַחֲפָצִים חָמְרִיִּם הֵן רִאשׁוֹנוֹת לְהַכִּיר אֶת פְּעָמָיו. תְּכוּנָתוֹ, הַמְּלֵאָה עִנְיָן לַחֲפָצִים חָמְרִיִּם, חֵפֶץ הָאָרֶץ, הָעֲבוֹדָה, הַסֵּדֶר וְהַמִּשְׁטָר הַחֶבְרָתִי, לֹא זָרָה הִיא לְרוּחָם כְּמוֹ לְרוּחַ בְּנֵי עֲלִיָּה הַמְיֻחָדִים שֶׁל עַם מְיֻשָּׁךְ וּמְמֹרָט אֲשֶׁר שָׁכַח חַיִּים וְנָשָׂה טוֹבָה. –

וְכָאן אַנְשֵׁי-לֵב נִתְבָּעִים לָבֹא לַעֲמֹד בַּמַּעֲרָכָה, לְחַזֵּק יָדַיִם רָפוֹת, לְרוֹמֵם רוּחַ כָּל מִתְיָאֵשׁ וּלְאַמֵּץ כָּל כּוֹשֵׁל, לִקְרֹא בְקוֹל גָּדוֹל: "צִיּוֹן, אַל יִרְפּוּ יָדָיִךְ!". הִנֵּה נִשְׁמַת אֱלֹהִים חַיִּים הָעֲלוּמָה, אֲשֶׁר יָשְׁבָה בְּסֵתֶר הַמַּדְרֵגָה בְּכָל יְמֵי הַגָּלוּת, הוֹלֶכֶת וּמִתְגַּלָּה. אֶת הוֹדָהּ וְיִפְעָתָהּ הֲלֹא לֹא תוּכַל לְגַלּוֹת רַק בְּעַמָּהּ הַחַי חַיִּים שְׁלֵמִים עַל אַדְמָתוֹ. כְּשֵׁם שֶׁאֵין הַשְּׁכִינָה שׁוֹרָה בְּאִישׁ יְחִידִי אֶלָּא עַל גִּבּוֹר וְעָשִׁיר וּבַעַל-קוֹמָה, אֶלָּא שֶׁכָּל זֶה לֹא יִסְכּוֹן מְאוּמָה בִּלְתִּי הַמַּעֲלוֹת הָרוּחָנִיּוֹת שֶׁל חָכְמָה וַעֲנָוָה, - כָּךְ אֵין הַשְּׁכִינָה הַכְּלָלִית שׁוֹרָה אֶלָּא בְּעַם מָלֵא גְבוּרָה, עֹשֶׁר, וְקוֹמְמִיּוּת, אֶלָּא שֶׁכָּל אֵלֶּה יִמְצְאוּ אֶת עֶרְכָּם רַק בְּהֵעָשׂוֹתָם בְּסִיסִים לְהָאוֹר הָרוּחָנִי הָאֱלֹהִי, הַמְמַלֵּא אוֹר ד' וְעָנְוַת-צֶדֶק.

בְּנֶפֶשׁ נִדְהָמָה וּבְבִרְכַּיִם כּוֹשְׁלוֹת מֵעֹצֶר רָעָה וְיָגוֹן, שֶׁל עֲקַת-אוֹיֵב וְשִׁפְלוּת נְדוּדִים, בְּאֶפֶס תִּקְוָה וְנִחוּמִים בְּאַדְמַת נֵכָר, בָּאוּ אֶל הָאָרֶץ פְּזוּרֵי-גוֹלָה, שְׂרִידִים יְחִידִים. עֵינֵיהֶם הַטְּרוּטוֹת, מֵרֹב

hearts and holy souls, they saw it yet did not recognize its strength and substance, until they turned around and there it was—revealing itself. Those tendrils of new life that were closest to material urges were the first to show perceptible traces. The desire for land, for physical work, for social organization were not strange to the most exalted spirits of this long-suffering people that had generally forgotten the ways of physical existence and that was indebted for its material support to others.

Now we need dauntless people to step forward. They must strengthen the weak of spirit, raise up the despairing, support the falling, and declare loudly, "Zion: do not give up!" The spirit of the living, hidden God, concealed throughout the exile is being revealed. It can fully appear only in a people living a holistic life on its own land. Just as with individuals, the divine presence rests only on one who is strong, self-sufficient, and dignified, as well as possessing spiritual qualities of wisdom and humility, so, too, the divine presence rests only on the people collectively when they are strong, materially self-sufficient, and upright (these qualities, however, find their true value when they serve as a basis for the flourishing of a godly spirit, filled with the light of righteous humility).

Dumbfounded of spirit, knees quaking from the oppression of enemies and humiliating wanderings,

אֲפֵלָה שֶׁל גּוֹלָה אַחַר גּוֹלָה, לֹא תּוּכַלְנָה עוֹד לִסְבּוֹל אֶת כָּל תֹּקֶף הָאוֹר הַגָּדוֹל הַזָּרוּעַ בָּאָרֶץ. הַקּוֹמָה עוֹד לֹא נִזְדַּקְּפָה, הָרוּחַ עוֹד לֹא נִתְעוֹדֵד, הַנְּשָׁמָה הָאֱלֹהִית עוֹד לֹא נִתְגַּלְּתָה בִּתְעוּפַת עֻזָּהּ. אֲבָל קַוִּים בּוֹדְדִים שֶׁל אוֹרָה פְּזוּרִים בְּכָל עֲבָרִים, הַקֵּץ-הַמְּגֻלֶּה הוֹלֵךְ וְקָרֵב, וְכָל אֲשֶׁר רוּחַ-ד' מְפַעֲמוֹ יָחוּשׁ לִהְיוֹת מֵהַבּוֹנִים הָרִאשׁוֹנִים הַבּוֹנִים אֶת בִּנְיַן הָאֻמָּה בְּאֶרֶץ-חֶמְדַּת-עוֹלָמִים!

כְּמוֹ שֶׁצְּעִירָה הִיא קוֹמְמוּת עַמֵּנוּ עַל אַדְמַת הַקֹּדֶשׁ; כְּמוֹ שָׁדַל וְקָטָן הוּא בְּנִינֵנוּ לְעֻמַּת תִּקְוָתֵנוּ הַגְּדוֹלָה, שֶׁהִיא נֶאְדֶּרֶת בְּיָמִין ד' רוֹמֵמָה "לִנְטֹעַ שָׁמַיִם וְלִיסֹד אָרֶץ וְלֵאמֹר לְצִיּוֹן עַמִּי אָתָּה," כֵּן דַּק וְחַלּוּשׁ הוּא הָרוּחַ הַמַּרְגָּשׁ בְּקִרְבֵּנוּ מֵרוֹמְמוּתָהּ שֶׁל אֶרֶץ-חֶמְדָּה. וַהֲדַר-כְּבוֹד אֵל הַמִּתְגַּלֶּה בִּקְדֻשַּׁת הַיּוֹבֵל וְהַשְּׁמִטָּה עַל אַדְמַת הַקֹּדֶשׁ, הַנּוֹתֵן עֹז וְתַעֲצוּמוֹת לָעָם, רַק מֵרָחוֹק עוֹד יֵרָאֶה לָנוּ. אָמְנָם מֵחַיּוֹת הֵן אֶת רוּחֵנוּ הַמִּצְוֹת-הַתְּלוּיוֹת-בָּאָרֶץ כַּמָּה שֶׁעוֹלֶה בְּיָדֵינוּ לְקַיֵּם מֵהֶן גַּם כָּעֵת, אִם כִּי עֲדַיִן אֵין לָנוּ שׁוּם דָּבָר בִּשְׁלֵמוּתוֹ. אֲבָל הַגִּיעָה הַשָּׁעָה לִתְחִיַּת הַתּוֹרָה הַמְכֻוֶּנֶת לְעֻמַּת תְּחִיַּת הָאָרֶץ: תַּלְמוּדָן שֶׁל

61. Isa. 56:12.

devoid of hope or consolation in the lands of strangers, scattered exiles started to arrive in the land. Bleary-eyed from all the darkness of exile after exile, it was hard for them to absorb the great light that they found sown in the land. Their stature is still not upright and their spirits not yet revived, and the spirit of God is not yet revealed in full force. But scattered shafts of spiritual life suggest that the revealed end is coming closer. All in whom the divine spirit resonates feel themselves to be among the pioneering builders who are constructing the nation's home in its beloved, eternal land.

The reestablishment of the people in its holy land is still young, and what has been built until now is minuscule compared to the grandeur of our hope, which is mantled in godly power—"I, who planted the skies and made firm the earth, have said to Zion, you are My people!"[61] So, too, the spiritual revival within us that is starting to raise up our precious country is small and weak. The glory that will appear when shmita and *yovel* are observed on the holy land still seem far away. Nonetheless, our spirits are lifted by what we *can* fulfill of the mitzvot that are connected to the land, even though what we have is still only partial. Now is the time to revive those aspects of

הַמִּצְוֹת-הַתְּלוּיוֹת-בָּאָרֶץ הֵחֵל לִהְיוֹת הוֹלֵךְ וְנֶחְשָׁב, לְכָל עַם ד׳ הַמַּפְנֶה פָּנָיו אֶל אַרְצוֹ בְּרוּחַ ד׳ אֲשֶׁר עָלָיו, - לְחוֹבָה קְדוֹשָׁה יֶתֶר עַל הַחוֹבָה הַכְּלָלִית הַמַּקֶּפֶת אֶת כָּל הַתּוֹרָה כֻּלָּהּ; וּבְיוֹתֵר הַחֵלָּה חוֹבָתוֹ לְהִגָּלוֹת עַל יוֹשְׁבֵי אַדְמַת-הַקֹּדֶשׁ.

תַּלְמוּד מֵבִיא לִידֵי מַעֲשֶׂה, שִׁנּוּן הַהֲלָכוֹת בְּבֵרוּר וְהַרְחָבָה, עֲשׂוֹת סְפָרִים וְהַרְבּוֹת מֶחְקָר בָּהֶן, מְבִיאִים אֶת הַהַכָּרָה וְהָאַהֲבָה אֶל הַמִּצְוֹת-הַתְּלוּיוֹת-בָּאָרֶץ, אֲשֶׁר נִשְׁכְּחוּ שְׁנוֹת-מֵאוֹת רַבּוֹת מִכְּלָלוּת הָאֻמָּה, וְאוֹר ד׳, שֶׁבְּכָל אוֹת וָאוֹת וּבְכָל פְּרָט וּפְרָט מִפְּרָטֶיהָ שֶׁל תּוֹרָה, מוֹפִיעַ וּמְעוֹרֵר אֶת חֵשֶׁק שְׁמִירָתָן בְּכָל פְּרָטֵיהֶן, וְהַכָּרַת צִדְקָן וּכְבוֹדָן הוֹלֶכֶת וּמִתְרַבָּה לְפִי הַגְדָּלַת תּוֹרָתָן וְהַאֲדָרָתָהּ.

וְהִנֵּה עַתָּה הִגִּיעָה שְׁנַת-הַשְּׁמִטָּה לְפִי מִנְיָן הַשָּׁנִים הַמֻּחְזָק אִתָּנוּ. מֵרוֹב דַּלּוּת מַצַּב יְשׁוּבֵנוּ בָּאָרֶץ הֶכְרֵחַ הוּא אָמְנָם לְהִסְתַּפֵּק ע״פ רוֹב בְּהוֹרָאַת-שָׁעָה, כַּאֲשֶׁר הִסְכַּם מֵאָז ע״פ גְּדוֹלֵי-הַדּוֹר, אֲשֶׁר

---

62. Talmud Bavli, Kiddushin 40b. "Learning is greater [than action] because learning leads to action." This is Rabbi Akiva's opinion, cited in the talmudic debate about whether study is greater than deeds. Through citing this source, Rav Kook expresses the hope that the study of shmita will lead to its fuller observance.

the Torah that speak precisely to the revival of the land: learning about the special mitzvot of the land is becoming more and more significant for all those of God's people who are focusing on what is happening in the land to which God's spirit has returned—where a special holiness must be reflected and revealed by those who are living here, above and beyond the demands that the rest of the Torah makes on us wherever we are.

"Learning leads to action."[62] Studying the halakhot to gain clarity and breadth of understanding, writing books, and expanding research all increase awareness and love of the mitzvot connected to the land, which were forgotten by most of the people for many centuries. The divine light that suffuses every letter of every detail of the Torah awakens in us a desire to carefully observe these commandments in their entirety. Consciousness of their justice and importance will grow as the study of the Torah concerning them becomes greater and more magnificent.

Now the shmita year has arrived (according to the reckoning that we have). Owing to the poor situation of our settlements in the land, we will have to make do with the temporary expedient that was endorsed some time

נִכְנְסוּ לְתוֹךְ עֹמֶק מַצַּב הַיִּשׁוּב הֶחָדָשׁ בְּאַרְצֵנוּ הַקְּדוֹשָׁה, וּבְהַרְגָּשָׁה
נֶאֱמָנָה חָדְרוּ אֶל עֶרְכּוֹ בֶּעָתִיד, בְּחוּשָׁם שֶׁלֹּא לָבוּז לְיוֹם-קְטַנּוֹת
וְלָדַעַת כִּי מֵאֵת ד' הָיְתָה זֹּאת, לָתֵת נִיר לְעַמּוֹ עַל אַדְמַת-קָדְשׁוֹ
לִהְיוֹת לְפֶתַח-תִּקְוָה וּצְמִיחַת-קֶרֶן-יְשׁוּעָה, שֶׁגְּדוֹלָה הִיא חוֹבָתֵנוּ
לְיַשֵּׁר אֶת מְסִלָּתָהּ, לְבִלְתִּי תִּפְגַּע מִכְשׁוֹלִים מִצַּד הַמִּצְווֹת-הַתְּלוּיּוֹת-
בָּאָרֶץ כְּכָל הָאֶפְשָׁרִי. וְאֵין הַקָּבָּ"ה בָּא בִּטְרוּנְיָא עִם בְּרִיּוֹתָיו, וְכָל
הַנֶּאֱמַר לְהָקֵל בִּמְקוֹם מִצְוָה דְרַבִּים וּבִמְקוֹם הֶפְסֵד מְרֻבֶּה וּשְׁעַת-
הַדְּחָק, - כָּל אֵלֶּה חָבְרוּ יַחַד בִּשְׁאֵלָה זוֹ בְּמִדָּה מְרֻבָּה כָּל-כָּךְ, עַד
שֶׁאֵין לָהּ דֻּגְמָא בְּכָל הַשְּׁאֵלוֹת אֲשֶׁר נִתְעוֹרְרוּ בְּיִשְׂרָאֵל בְּחֵקֶר דִּין
וּמִשְׁפָּט, בְּכָל מֶשֶׁךְ הַגָּלוּת הָאֲרֻכָּה. אֲבָל לַמְרוֹת הַפְקָעַת-הַמִּצְוָה
אֲשֶׁר בְּהוֹרָאַת-שָׁעָה זוֹ יֶשְׁנָם כַּמָּה גוּפֵי-הֲלָכוֹת, הַנִּדְרָשִׁים לִשְׁמוֹר
וְלַעֲשׂוֹת בְּפֹעַל. גַּם נִמְצָאִים יִרְאֵי ד' הַחֲרֵדִים אֶל דְּבָרוֹ מְאֹד, אֲשֶׁר
מִפְּנֵי קְדֻשַּׁת חִבַּת-הַמִּצְווֹת-הַתְּלוּיּוֹת-בָּאָרֶץ וּמִצְוַת הַשְּׁבִיעִית,
שֶׁעֵינֵי כָּל יִשְׂרָאֵל נְשׂוּאוֹת לְקִיּוּמָהּ בְּאֶרֶץ-חֶמְדָּה, אֵינָם חָסִים עַל

63. Rav Kook refers here to the *heter mekhira* device of selling the land for the duration of the shmita.

64. Hosea 2:17. Rav Kook quotes from the passage that likens Israel's turn to idolatry to a woman's adultery, which he has previously cited in his introduction. This verse describes the lovers' reconciliation. In Hebrew, the phrase is *petah tikva*, which was the name given to one of the first modern agricultural settlements in Israel (founded in 1878) for similar reasons.

65. Ps. 118:23.

ago by the greatest authorities of the generation, who understood deeply the situation of the new settlement in our holy land.[63] They had a penetrating sense of what it could become in the future and knew not to belittle its smallness because they understood that plowing these first furrows on our land could be a "gateway of hope"[64] for our people and portend the growth of a salvation that "came from the Lord."[65] They realized their historical obligation to smooth the path of the new settlements and, as much as possible, not to let the mitzvot that are connected to the land be obstacles. God does not make tyrannical and unreasonable demands of His creatures. The circumstances that allow us to be lenient regarding mitzvot pertaining to the whole community when there is the likelihood of significant financial loss, or in a temporary situation of acute need, are all compounded in this case to an extent unparalleled in the annals of legal questions that have arisen throughout our lengthy exile. Despite the suspension of the mitzvah (of shmita) that is entailed by this temporary edict, there are still

הֶפְסֵד וָטֹרַח וְהֵם נְכוֹנִים לְקַיְּמָהּ בְּכָל כֹּחַ, - כַּדִּין וְכַמִּשְׁפָּט. בְּרוּכִים יִהְיוּ לַד' וּלְעַמּוֹ.

וְלֹבַד-זֶה הַתַּלְמוּד בְּעַצְמוֹ יָבִיא לִידֵי מַעֲשֶׂה, שִׁנּוּן הַהֲלָכוֹת יַחֲקֹק בִּלְבָבוֹת אֶת חִיּוּבָם בְּלֵב וּמִשְׁמַטָּה לַשְּׁמִטָּה יִתְוַסְּפוּ רַבִּים, אֲשֶׁר בְּעֹז ד' בִּלְבָבָם יַרְחִיבוּ אֶת גְּבוּל הַמִּצְוָה בְּכָל הַרְחָבָתָהּ וּפְרָטֶיהָ, וּבְשִׂמְחַת יִשְׂרָאֵל בְּעוֹשָׂיו בְּהַר-הַקֹּדֶשׁ הָעֹז וְהַהִתְעַצְּמוּת אֲשֶׁר לְעַם-ד' בֶּעָתִיד יוֹסִיפוּ אֶת הַיְכֹלֶת לְקִיּוּמָהּ הַגָּמוּר וְהַמְשֻׁכְלָל.

מֵרוּחַ ד' הַחוֹפֵף עַל עַמּוֹ וְאַרְצוֹ תָּחֵל קְדֻשַּׁת הַשְּׁמִטָּה וְתִפְאֶרֶת זִיו כְּבוֹדָהּ לְהִתְפַּשֵּׁט עַל כָּל רוּחַ וָנֶפֶשׁ, לְכָל עַם ד' וּבְיִחוּד לַיּוֹשְׁבִים בְּצֵל קֹדֶשׁ שֶׁל אֶרֶץ חֶמְדָּה, וּבִנְעִימַת-יְדִידוּת עֹז אַהֲבָתָהּ. וְרוּחַ קָדְשַׁת הַיּוֹבֵל הַמִּסְתַּתֵּר יוֹפִיעַ מֵאוֹצַר קָדְשׁוֹ עַל קְדֻשַּׁת הַשְּׁמִטָּה, לְעוֹרֵר קֶרֶן יְשׁוּעָה וְקוֹל שׁוֹפָר לְשַׂגֵּב יֶשַׁע, לְעוֹרֵר יְשֵׁנִים וּלְעוֹדֵד גְּאוּלִים. –

---

66.   Jerusalem. See, e.g., Isa. 56:7.

some halakhot pertaining to shmita that we are required to observe. And those who are especially God-fearing, whose holy love of the mitzvot connected to the land that we have long yearned to observe is so great, are not deterred by the trouble and loss they may incur through fully observing shmita as it should be—and they shall be blessed!

In addition, learning itself leads to action. Studying the halakhot will engrave them on our hearts. From one shmita year to the next, more and more people will be caught up with enthusiasm. With godly boldness in their hearts, they will broaden the fulfillment of the mitzvah in all its details. The fierce joy that will be generated by Israel observing the shmita on the holy mountain[66] will lead, in the future, to its complete and all-encompassing fulfillment.

The holiness of shmita will emanate from the spirit of God that hovers over His people and land and spread to all life—to all God's people and especially to those who live in the holy shelter of this precious land, in the sweet companionship of its loving refuge. The spirit of the Jubilee, which lies latent, will appear from within the storehouse of holiness that is in the shmita, and the sound of the shofar will herald salvation, rousing the sleepy and encouraging the recently redeemed.

לְזֹאת מָצָאתִי לִי חוֹבָה לְהוֹצִיא אֶת הַחִבֶּרֶת הַזֹּאת, אֲשֶׁר סִדַּרְתִּיהָ
לְהִלְכוֹת שְׁבִיעִית בע"ה. אֲקַנֶּה לִשְׁמוֹ ית' כִּי יַגְדִּיל תּוֹרָה וְיַאְדִיר
וִיזַכֶּה אוֹתִי וְאֶת כָּל לְמוּדֵי-ד', וּבְיוֹתֵר אֶת אַחַי אֲשֶׁר אֶקְרָא לָהֶם
נֹעַם אֵלּוּ תַּלְמִידֵי-חֲכָמִים שֶׁבְּאֶרֶץ יִשְׂרָאֵל לְהַרְחִיב דְּבָרִים עַל
הַמִּצְוֹת-הַתְּלוּיוֹת-בָּאָרֶץ בִּכְלָל וְעַל מִצְוַת שְׁבִיעִית בִּפְרָט. וְיַחַד
עִם הָעֵסֶק בַּהֲלָכוֹת הַמַּעֲשִׂיוֹת יִתְכּוֹנֵן הַלֵּב בְּטוּב-טַעַם-וָדַעַת
לְהַשְׂכִּיל בְּנֹעַם ד' בְּאוֹר דַּעַת אֱלֹהִים, בְּרוּחַ מָלֵא עֵצָה וּגְבוּרָה,
וְהַחוֹנֵן לְאָדָם דַּעַת הַנּוֹתֵן אוֹר חָכְמָה עַל אַדְמַת קָדְשׁוֹ, אֲשֶׁר זָכִינוּ
לְהִסְתּוֹפֵף בְּחֶבֶל נַחֲלָתוֹ, יְמַלְּאֵנוּ רוּחַ דֵּעָה וִיחַזְּקֵנוּ בְּשֵׂכֶל טוֹב,
וְיַצִּילֵנוּ מִכָּל שְׁגִיאָה, לְמַעַן עַמּוֹ וְנַחֲלָתוֹ.

וּמְהֵרָה יֵאָמְנוּ דְּבָרָיו דִּנְבִיאוֹ:

"וְלָקַחְתִּי אֶתְכֶם מִן-הַגּוֹיִם וְקִבַּצְתִּי אֶתְכֶם מִכָּל-הָאֲרָצוֹת וְהֵבֵאתִי
אֶתְכֶם אֶל-אַדְמַתְכֶם. וְזָרַקְתִּי עֲלֵיכֶם מַיִם טְהוֹרִים וּטְהַרְתֶּם מִכֹּל
טֻמְאוֹתֵיכֶם וּמִכָּל-גִּלּוּלֵיכֶם אֲטַהֵר אֶתְכֶם. וְנָתַתִּי לָכֶם לֵב חָדָשׁ
וְרוּחַ חֲדָשָׁה אֶתֵּן בְּקִרְבְּכֶם וַהֲסִרֹתִי אֶת-לֵב הָאֶבֶן מִבְּשַׂרְכֶם וְנָתַתִּי
לָכֶם לֵב בָּשָׂר. וְאֶת-רוּחִי אֶתֵּן בְּקִרְבְּכֶם וְעָשִׂיתִי אֵת אֲשֶׁר-בְּחֻקַּי

That is why I felt obliged to write this book laying out the halakhot of shmita, with God's help.

I hope to God that through it, the Torah will be made great and glorious; that I and all those who yearn to learn of God's ways, especially my brothers, whom I call upon in pleasantness, the great Torah scholars of the Land of Israel, will merit to expand our teaching about the mitzvot that concern the land, and especially shmita. And alongside our involvement in the practical halakhot, may our hearts be strengthened with wisdom and discernment to know, with a spirit that is filled with counsel and strength, the light of divine knowledge that is being granted to our holy land, which we have been fortunate to inherit; and may this spirit of this knowledge fill and strengthen us with sound understanding and save us from errors for the sake of His name and inheritance.

May God's word to the prophets be soon fulfilled:

"I will take you from among the nations and gather you from all countries, and I will bring you back to your land. I will sprinkle clean water upon you and you shall be clean: I will cleanse you from all your uncleanness and all your fetishes. And I will give you a new heart and put a new spirit into you: I will remove the heart of stone from

תֵּלֵכוּ וּמִשְׁפָּטַי תִּשְׁמְרוּ וַעֲשִׂיתֶם. וִישַׁבְתֶּם בָּאָרֶץ אֲשֶׁר נָתַתִּי לַאֲבֹתֵיכֶם וִהְיִיתֶם לִי לְעָם וְאָנֹכִי אֶהְיֶה לָכֶם לֵאלֹהִים. וְהוֹשַׁעְתִּי אֶתְכֶם מִכֹּל טֻמְאוֹתֵיכֶם וְקָרָאתִי אֶל-הַדָּגָן וְהִרְבֵּיתִי אֹתוֹ וְלֹא-אֶתֵּן עֲלֵיכֶם רָעָב. וְהִרְבֵּיתִי אֶת פְּרִי הָעֵץ וּתְנוּבַת הַשָּׂדֶה לְמַעַן אֲשֶׁר לֹא תִקְחוּ עוֹד חֶרְפַּת רָעָב בַּגּוֹיִם."

"כֹּה אָמַר ד' אֱלֹהִים בְּיוֹם טַהֲרִי אֶתְכֶם מִכֹּל עֲוֹנוֹתֵיכֶם וְהוֹשַׁבְתִּי אֶת הֶעָרִים וְנִבְנוּ הֶחֳרָבוֹת. וְהָאָרֶץ הַנְּשַׁמָּה תֵּעָבֵד תַּחַת אֲשֶׁר הָיְתָה שְׁמָמָה לְעֵינֵי כָּל עוֹבֵר. וְאָמְרוּ הָאָרֶץ הַלֵּזוּ הַנְּשַׁמָּה הָיְתָה כְּגַן עֵדֶן וְהֶעָרִים הֶחֳרֵבוֹת וְהַנְשַׁמּוֹת וְהַנֶּהֱרָסוֹת בְּצוּרוֹת יָשָׁבוּ. וְיָדְעוּ הַגּוֹיִם אֲשֶׁר יִשָּׁאֲרוּ סְבִיבוֹתֵיכֶם כִּי אֲנִי ד' בָּנִיתִי הַנֶּהֱרָסוֹת נָטַעְתִּי הַנְּשַׁמָּה אֲנִי ד' דִּבַּרְתִּי וְעָשִׂיתִי."

עיה"ק יפו ת"ו, התר"ע

your body and give you a heart of flesh; and I will put My spirit into you. Thus I will cause you to follow My laws and faithfully to observe My rules. Then you shall dwell in the land that I gave to your father, and you shall be My people and I will be your God. And when I have delivered you from all your uncleanness, I will summon the grain and make it abundant, and I will not bring famine upon you. I will make the fruit of your trees and the crops of your fields abundant, so that you shall never again be humiliated before the nations because of the famine."[67]

"Thus said the Lord, God: when I have cleansed you of all your iniquities, I will people your settlements, and the ruined places shall be rebuilt; and the desolate land, after laying waste in the sight of every passerby, shall again be tilled. And men shall say, 'That land, once desolate, has now become like the garden of Eden; and the cities, once ruined, desolate, and ravaged, are now populated and fortified.' And the nations that are left around you shall know that I the Lord have rebuilt the ravaged places and replanted the desolate land. I the Lord have spoken and will act."[68]

The holy city of Jaffa, may it be built and established, 1909.

67. Ezek. 36:24–30.
68. Ezek. 36:33–36.

SHMITA FOR THE FUTURE:
CYCLING TOWARD A RENEWED VISION OF LAND AND SOCIETY

Shabbat Ha'aretz was the most detailed and systematic argument ever published in support of the *heter mekhira* and had the effect of institutionalizing the practice. After Rav Kook became the first chief rabbi of Palestine (in 1921), the chief rabbinate began to organize the shmita-year sale of the land for the whole community and continued to do so after the foundation of the State of Israel in 1948.

The anti–*heter mekhira* ranks were strengthened in 1933, when Rabbi Avraham Yeshaya Karelitz (1878–1953), known by the name of his great halakhic work, the Ḥazon Ish, immigrated to Israel and became the unofficial leader of the Ḥaredi community there. On the eve of the 1937–38 shmita, the Ḥazon Ish wrote a lengthy critique of Rav Kook's arguments (after the latter's death and, contrary to the usual rabbinic practice, without ever mentioning his opponent by name).

The Ḥazon Ish believed that the Torah prohibition of selling land in Israel to non-Jews (Deut. 7:1–2) was an insurmountable obstacle to the *heter mekhira*. He rejected Rav Kook's meta-halakhic arguments that since the future of Jewish settlement in Israel was at stake, the halakhah needed to be lenient. According to the Ḥazon Ish, "all of the murmurings that this is a situation of danger that demands lifesaving measures derives only from coldheartedness and a lack of the respect due to the performance of the Torah and its precepts."[1] The Ḥazon Ish denied Rav Kook's core premise that it was not feasible to observe shmita in Israel. His constituency consisted not of the whole nation but of God-fearing farmers who were willing to sacrifice for the sake of the mitzvot; if they could observe shmita properly and survive, that was sufficient for the Ḥazon Ish to demonstrate that shmita observance was feasible.

The battle lines were drawn; the Ḥazon Ish's position on *heter mekhira* is the Ḥaredi position until today. During the shmita, his followers eat produce that is imported, grown by Arabs, or they rely on the *otzar beit din* method. Most Religious Zionist Jews rely on the *heter mekhira*. Most secular and traditional Jews do, too, without caring much either way, because the official Israeli chief rabbinate (the Rabanut) follows the *heter mekhira*, which is the official position of the Israeli government.

Until the shmita of 2007–08, the Rabanut gave its kosher certification to all *heter mekhira* produce—indeed, it performed the sale on behalf of interested farmers. In 2007, however, the Ḥaredi rabbi Yonah Metzger was head of the Rabanut. Bowing to pressure from other Ḥaredi leaders, he announced that any Rabanut-employed city rabbi who did not support the *heter* was

---

1 *Igerot Ḥazon Ish* (Collection of the letters of the Ḥazon Ish) (Hebrew) (B'nei Brak: Greineman, 1990), 3:85.

allowed to revoke the kosher certification of any restaurants and hotels in his city that bought *heter mekhira* produce.

Metzger created an absurd situation in which the body that implemented the *heter* could also refuse to recognize it. As non–*heter mekhira* produce is more expensive, this ruling could have spelled financial disaster for many. The Tzohar group of Religious Zionist rabbis announced that they would flout the chief rabbinate and issue *heter mekhira* certificates in cities where the local rabbis would not. Rabbi Rafi Feuerstein, chairman of Tzohar, said: "We believe it is important to strengthen Jewish farmers and provide reasonably priced produce to the Jewish nation." Rabbi David Stav of Tzohar said: "We are trying to save the chief rabbinate from itself."[2]

Israel's supreme court intervened, ruling in October 2007 that the Rabanut may not revoke the *heter mekhira* without a public process allowing farmers and others affected to be heard. Such a radical change of a century-old policy could not take place by fiat, the court declared. The *New York Times* covered the story, and I was interviewed on NPR about the controversy, doing my best to put a sympathetic gloss on these shenanigans.

Confusion and anger reigned, and the halakhah and the rabbis were ridiculed. The episode was further proof, if any was required, that the chief rabbinate was Rav Kook's least successful creation. In a painful historical irony, the chief rabbinate that Rav

---

2 Both quotations from Steven Erlanger, "As Farmers and Fields Rest, a Land Grows Restless," *New York Times*, October 8, 2007.

Kook built undermined the *heter mekhira* that he did more than anyone to promote.

Shmita: 2014–15 and Beyond

Shabbat Ha'aretz instituted a paradoxical status quo that persisted for a century, whereby shmita was observed in Israel primarily by avoiding its observance. Rav Kook compounded the paradox by publishing the halakhic argument of *Shabbat Ha'aretz*, which legitimated effectively avoiding the observance of shmita, together with a non-halakhic introduction that elucidated the extraordinary potential socioeconomic and spiritual significance of shmita when fully observed.

The status quo of shmita observance/nonobservance in Israel that has endured for 100 years, since the publication of *Shabbat Ha'aretz*, is crumbling. It is being eroded from two opposite sides. On the one hand, it is undermined by Ḥaredi control of the Israeli chief rabbinate, which dislikes the *heter mekhira* and served notice in 2007 of its intention to withdraw support for the *heter*. On the other hand, a wave of grassroots initiatives comprising environmentalists, economists, social activists, and innovative religious thinkers, crossing communal-denominational lines and inspired partly by the 2011 social justice protests, is looking for ways to actively observe shmita rather than avoid its observance. These initiatives seek to actualize the powerful teachings and values that they find in shmita, relating to sustainable agriculture, debt relief, the economic commons, social justice, and much more, in the complex socioeconomic reality of twenty-first-century Israel.

The shmita year of 2014–15 looks set to be a watershed in shmita observance, with the institutional status quo coming under unprecedented pressure and, simultaneously, a plethora of innovative, grassroots-led, religiously meaningful, and socioeconomically significant ways of observing shmita starting to emerge. Projects in Israel and the U.S. are connecting shmita to debt forgiveness, social justice, and sustainable agriculture. A veteran of the Israeli technology sector, Yossi Tsuria, has developed a list of forty-nine ways to enact the values of shmita in the hi-tech sector.[3] The Israeli government is poised to sponsor significant shmita initiatives spanning debt relief, education, and environmental conservation. Projects pioneered by Sova, Hazon, Teva Ivri, and other organizations are aiming to show how shmita addresses core, seemingly intractable, socioeconomic challenges that we all face: the growing polarization of wealth and poverty, our ceaseless exploitation of human and natural capital, and our very limited ability to predict, regulate, and moderate the periodic cyclical crashes to which the economy seems prone.

An extraordinary event held at the Knesset on January 6, 2014, showcased how different the coming shmita could be. Knesset members and ministers spanning the political spectrum, left and right, religious and secular, spoke in support of measures that will publicly implement broad values of shmita in Israeli government policy. Several declared that the shameful politicking

---

3 For a summary, see http://blogs.timesofisrael.com/shmittah-in-hi-tech.

and public ridicule of the rabbinate in the last cycle had spurred them to want to restore the dignity of shmita by enacting its real values. The leader of the opposition, Isaac Herzog (grandson of Rav Yitzhak Herzog, who succeeded Rav Kook as Ashkenazi chief rabbi), spoke passionately about the rich resources in Jewish tradition for renewing socioeconomic thought, shmita foremost among them; Ruth Calderon, a Talmud educator who became a Knesset member (and who sponsored the gathering), declared the potential of shmita to unite different factions of Israel society.

The government's chief economic adviser, Professor Eugene Kandel (a secular Russian immigrant to Israel), delivered a *shiur* on moral hazard and the *prozbul*; the education minister, Shai Piron, spoke about how all Israel's schoolchildren would learn about the socioeconomic and environmental values of shmita in the coming year; the environment minister, Amir Peretz, announced measures to fund a moratorium on fishing in the Sea of Galilee during the shmita year. Stocks have been almost exhausted by overfishing, but a year of respite would restore them to previous levels. Peretz also announced plans to open Israel's national parks free of charge in the shmita year, enacting the idea of the commons, while the Ministry of Welfare unveiled a planned fund of 70 million shekels to enable 10,000 Israelis to escape crushing debt this shmita, in a joint initiative with major banks, utilities, and NGOs. Rabbi Yoel Bin Nun, a veteran Religious Zionist rabbi and shmita activist, shook his head and declared that all this energy, activity, and cross-party cooperation around the issue of shmita was nothing short of miraculous.

Knesset member Shuli Meulam of the Jewish Home Party projected onto a screen passages from this book—the introduction to Rav Kook's *Shabbat Ha'aretz*—and, together with her Knesset colleagues and the assembled public, studied them—a powerful prism through which to frame and understand the fluid, unstable, yet potentially highly creative reality of the 2014–15 shmita.

Indeed, one way to understand the potential significance of the coming shmita year is as slippage in the unstable relationship between the halakhic and aggadic parts of *Shabbat Ha'aretz*. The halakhic piece—the *heter mekhira* as a necessary device in a provisional reality—is under attack, while the aggadic vision of the book's introduction, of how shmita might ideally be observed, is beginning to blossom. As Rav Kook writes in the introduction, the effect of shmita is cumulative over seven cycles. If the 2014–15 year indeed marks the beginning of a new approach to shmita, then may the 2063–64 year see its culmination in ways that we cannot yet imagine.

Yehudah Mirsky puts his finger on a central problem in Rav Kook's thought. Kook believed that he was living in pre-messianic times and that the return to Israel that he witnessed in his day was the beginning of the redemption. Noting that Rav Kook's followers have tended to flatten his complex, dialectic thinking, Mirsky suggests that not all the blame for this can be justly laid at the students' door; this messianic strain in Rav Kook's thought does provide a constant temptation to oversimplification through collapsing the delicate tension between the imperfect now and the dreamed-of future: "Thus, one of the key questions about Rav Kook's place in future Jewish thought is whether the structure of his ideas is entirely dependent on messianic energy to hold all its contradictions together, and just how long that apotheosis can be deferred."[4]

Shmita is an interesting test case for Mirsky's question. Rav Kook, like Maimonides before him,[5] suggested that full realization of the soaring ideals of shmita and the Jubilee will be part of the messianic era. Can Rav Kook's thinking in *Shabbat Ha'aretz* continue to inspire practical steps toward a richer realization of shmita that falls short of the messianic culmination, yet brings it tangibly closer to fulfillment?

---

4 Yehudah Mirsky, *Rav Kook: Mystic in a Time of Revolution* (New Haven, Conn.: Yale University Press, 2014), 237–38.

5 Maimonides, *Mishne Torah, Hilkhot Melakhim*, 11:1.

ACKNOWLEDGMENTS

It is a pleasure to thank Nigel Savage, director of Hazon, for his visionary initiative in suggesting and sponsoring this book; Jorian Polis Schutz for his enthusiastic and insightful support; Elisheva Urbas for her intelligent and meticulous editing, keeping me close to the rules wherever possible while helping avoid various barbarities; Janice Meyerson for her excellent copyediting; Jessica Sacks for generous and helpful comments; Richard Resnick, from whom I first heard of Rav Kook's extraordinary body of thought; Rabbi Hillel Rachmani for his profound lectures on this thought at Yeshivat Har Etzion; Professor Benjamin Ish-Shalom for his rigorous and inspiring introductory course on Rav Kook at Beit Morasha; Professor Yehudah Mirsky for giving me prepublication sight of his superb new biography of Rav Kook; Dr. Michael Kagan for years of encouragement and stimulating conversations about Judaism, economics, and the environment; Yosef Abramowitz and Weldon Turner for encouraging me to bring this book into conversation with our work at Energiya Global; and my wife, Yaffa Aranoff, for her close reading, broad knowledge of Jewish mystical writings, and general, incalculable support.

READINGS AND RESOURCES

 ## Life of Rav Kook

Rav Kook: Mystic in a Time of Revolution, by Yehudah Mirsky (Yale University Press, 2014)

Abraham Isaac Kook: The Lights of Penitence, anthology of Rav Kook's writings, trans. Ben Zion Bokser (Paulist Press, 1978)

Rav Avraham Itzhak HaCohen Kook: Between Rationalism and Mysticism, by Benjamin Ish-Shalom, trans. Ora Wiskind-Elper (SUNY Press, 1993)

The World of Rav Kook's Thought, ed. Benjamin Ish-Shalom and Shalom Rosenberg (Avi Chai, 1991)

 ## Shmita and Jewish Life

Hazon Shmita Sourcebook
A 120-page sourcebook tracking the evolution of shmita through Jewish texts from ancient times to today
hazon.org/shmita

"Re-Pacing and (Self)-Renewal," by Dr. Jeremy Benstein
Explores the idea of sustainability through the tenets of shmita
hazon.org/wp-content/uploads/2013/07/Re-Pacing-and-Self-Renewal_Benstein.pdf

Envisioning Sabbatical Culture: A Shmita Manifesto, by Yigal Deutscher
A 60-page booklet of poetic visioning and illustrations that weaves language and art into a shmita dreamscape
7seedsproject.org/manifesto

"Shemita as a Foundation for Jewish Ecological Education," by Nati Passow (Coalition for the Advancement of Jewish Education [CAJE], 2008)
Exhibits the transformative power of shmita as an educational tool
www.bjpa.org/publications/downloadPublication cfm?PublicationID=4789

"Toward a Jubilee Economy & Ecology in the Modern World," by Rabbi Arthur Waskow
A chapter from Waskow's book *Godwrestling: Round 2* (Jewish Lights, 1996)
theshalomcenter.org/node/1396

 Ways to Get Involved

Shmita Project

An online platform created to connect individuals and organizations across the world interested in exploring shmita and infusing all aspects of the Jewish community with the values and ideals found in the shmita year

hazon.org/shmita
facebook.com/shmitaproject

7 Seeds

A set of contemporary educational tools to celebrate ancient Jewish wisdom teachings as a path toward designing and activating local community, sustainable agriculture, and financial equality

7seedsproject.org

Sova Project

A shared endeavor created as a space for conversation surrounding issues of sustainability, with a particular focus on economic justice

sovaproject.org

Teva Ivri Israeli Shmita Project

Promotes Jewish environmental responsibility and utilizes the environmental and social values rooted in the Jewish tradition as the foundational building blocks of Israeli culture and society

tevaivri.org.il

JEWISH INSPIRATION. SUSTAINABLE COMMUNITIES.

The word *hazon* means "vision."

We work to create a healthier and more sustainable Jewish community and a healthier and more sustainable world for all.

Our motto is "*the Torah is a commentary on the world, and the world is a commentary on the Torah,*" which reflects our determination to apply Jewish thought to some of the greatest challenges of our time—and our belief that the act of doing so is good not only for the world but also for the renewal of Jewish life itself.

We effect change in three ways:

- Through **transformative experiences,** such as immersive multi-day programs that directly touch people's lives in powerful ways;
- Through **thought leadership** that is changing the world through the power of new ideas and fresh thinking. We include in this category writing, teaching, curriculum development, and advocacy, among other things;
- And through **capacity building**, which means not just working with people as individuals but explicitly supporting and networking great projects and partners in North America and Israel.

We were founded in 2000 and have grown every year since. We are based in New York City and at the Isabella Freedman Jewish Retreat Center in Falls Village, Connecticut, and we have staff in San Francisco, San Diego, Boulder, Denver, and Philadelphia. We welcome participants of all religious backgrounds and none, and we work closely with a wide range of institutions and leaders across the Jewish world and beyond.

As part of our ongoing work to create healthier and more sustainable communities in the Jewish world and beyond, Hazon is working with various partners, including the Siach Network and organizations in the UK and Israel, to reignite a conversation about sabbatical culture ahead of the next full shmita cycle (2015-2022).

Also available from Hazon

Learn more: www.hazon.org/education

Food for Thought: Hazon's Sourcebook on Jews, Food & Contemporary Life

A 130-page sourcebook that draws on texts from within and beyond Jewish traditions to explore a range of topics relating to Jews and food.

Hazon Food Audit and Food Guide Toolkit

A seven-chapter, easy-to-use assessment tool that helps you to identify the strengths and weaknesses of your institution's food practices and develop an action plan to make your institution healthier and more sustainable.

Healthy and Sustainable Shabbat and Holiday Guides

Celebrate the Jewish holidays in line with your values. Inspire a theme for a holiday, an activity for your family, or an event for your community.

Tu b'Shvat Seder and Sourcebook

A reimagined Tu b'Shvat haggadah with new texts, discussion questions, and activities to bring this ancient holiday into your home.

שַׁבָּת הָאָרֶץ